WeRe You RaiseD by WolVes?

ALSO BY CHRISTIE MELLOR

The Three-Martini Playdate
The Three-Martini Family Vacation

An Imprint of HarperCollinsPublishers

HarperCollins books may be purchased for educational, business, or sales promotional use. For information please write: Special Markets Department, HarperCollins Publishers, 10 East 53rd Street, New York, NY 10022.

FIRST EDITION

Designed by Susan Walsh

Library of Congress Cataloging-in-Publication Data has been applied for.

ISBN 978-0-06-123824-6

08 09 10 11 12   OV/RRD   10 9 8 7 6 5 4 3 2 1

To my very own kind and thoughtful slackers, Edison and Atticus.
I love you both more than I can say.

Now, please go make your beds.

Contents

Hello, brand-new grown-up! You may be just out of college, or maybe you didn't go, or are just about to go. You may be looking for a job. You may already have one, maybe a really good one, maybe one better than mine or your high school history teacher's. You are living on your own, and more things are expected of you, which can be annoying, because the fact is, you still secretly wish your mom would come over and clean your kitchen and do your laundry. Perhaps you wish this not so secretly. Your mom may, in fact, still be cleaning your kitchen and doing your laundry. Which is very nice of her. But it's something you'll need to learn to do yourself, sooner or later. Preferably sooner. I mean, really.

There may be a great many things that seem like curious, old-world holdovers from a quaint time long ago, things you think you really don't ever need to know. You may think you don't need to know them, but knowing them will really make you a much more well-rounded and all-around more charming person.

I'm sure that as a young adult, you don't want to be mistaken for an overindulged, ill-mannered brat, but there seem to be an alarming number of young adults who appear to be as helpless and self-centered as toddlers, and often with the same lack of manners. It might have been amusing, even adorable, when they were three, but they are twenty-seven, and don't know how to make a bed, or write a thank-you note, or boil an egg.

Yes, it's important to eat well and exercise, but I hear young women talking about the fat content of their food at an otherwise delightful dinner party, or discussing the amount of carbohydrates they must no longer ingest for fear of ballooning. Women, discussing ballooning, just as I am about to tuck into a perfectly lovely plate of pasta in a light cream sauce. Honestly, the brainpower required to count daily fat grams could be used keeping up with current events, or learning to speak Italian. Cut in half the long hours spent at the gym every day. Catch up on your Tolstoy and George Eliot, exercising some of those dormant brain muscles.

In addition to gaining valuable survival skills, you may come to a better understanding of the true meaning of etiquette. Etiquette is not so much about knowing how to use a fish fork, although that information might come in handy at some point; it is really more about putting other people at ease. By making the people around you comfortable, and therefore forgetting about yourself for a few minutes, you are actually helping society run more smoothly and in a much more enjoyable manner. You are greasing the wheels of social discourse. Yes, you have all that power in your hot little hands. You have the power to smooth the rough social edges, to help people feel more relaxed, to make the world fall in love—with each other, and possibly, with you.

Perhaps I've overstated it. But I doubt it. So let's take stock. It's time to set down that bottle of expensive water, review some simple rules of etiquette, and take a few totally random tips that will help you get through life without irritating too many people.

WeRe You Raised by WOLVes?

Home Sweet Home

MAKE YOUR BED!

Yes, it seems like a simple concept. And no, I am not your mother. I can't really *make* you make your bed. I understand, really I do. You are on your own, and no one, blessedly, is there to tell you to make your bed and pick up your t-shirt from the floor. It's your apartment, why shouldn't you leave your bed unmade? You're going to be out anyway—maybe all day, maybe all night. And why does it need to be made every day, anyway? You're only going to be sleeping in it again tonight.

But there is an idea used in law enforcement called the "broken window" theory that holds that if there is a broken window on a building, and if it is not immediately fixed, then it sends a signal to the neighborhood that nobody really cares. Vermin move into the building, graffiti springs up overnight, and garbage is dumped on the doorstep. More windows are broken. So, along those lines, I am suggesting that if you leave your bed constantly unmade, it sends a signal (to you) that it's also okay to leave your stinky socks on the floor, your dirty sweatpants slung over the chair, and a moldy crust of pizza sitting on top of a stack of magazines. You may think you're the sort that would never dream of leaving food lying around, but these things creep up on you, just like that broken window. You leave the bed unmade for too long, and pretty soon you find yourself sitting in a pool of your own waste, eating out of a takeout container in front of reality show reruns. If you jumped out of bed every morning and just *made your bed*, then it would be done, and it would put into stark relief the other spots that you could, in fact, neaten up just for the sake of possible visitors, a sense of esthetics, and the betterment of humanity in general.

How?

The easiest way to make a bed is to sleep in a completely maintenance-free bed to begin with, as they do in Europe. Simply cover your bed with some sort of down-filled duvet, which will require nothing more than fluffing and straightening once you pop out of bed, and easily camouflages any lumps or stray Underoos that might be stuck under the covers.

However, you may have heard your mother, or grandmother, or some ancient, eccentric aunt discussing "hospital corners" or "hospital folds," or reminiscing wistfully about beds off of which one could "bounce a quarter." Aren't you curious? Haven't you always secretly wanted to know what a hospital corner is, anyway? Doesn't it carry a vague suggestion of stern, unsmiling, yet beautiful women in starched white uniforms, coming at you with thermometers and bedpans? No, you say, with a slightly worried look on your face. You have no idea what I'm talking about. But someday you might be visiting a friend, or a relative, and you'll be staying in their guest room. And this kind friend or relative who has put you up for the night, or for three days, won't have a bulky duvet bedspread. You will need to know how to properly make the bed. You will need to uncover the mysteries of a hospital corner.

It could be just another bit of trivia to add to your store of knowledge, but in case you haven't yet made your life easier by purchasing a fat duvet and simply have been putting up with a messy, half-made bed, here is how a standard American bed is made: Place the fitted bottom sheet, the one with the elastic thingys on the corners, over the corners of your mattress. Tug it and smooth it out, until you have a vast expanse of unwrinkled sheet.

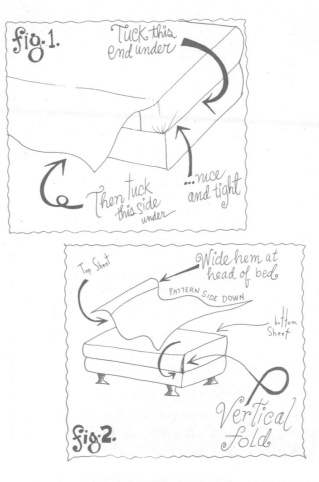

fig. 1.

Tuck this end under

...nice and tight

Then tuck this side under

fig. 2.

Top Sheet

Wide hem at head of bed

PATTERN SIDE DOWN

bottom Sheet

Vertical fold

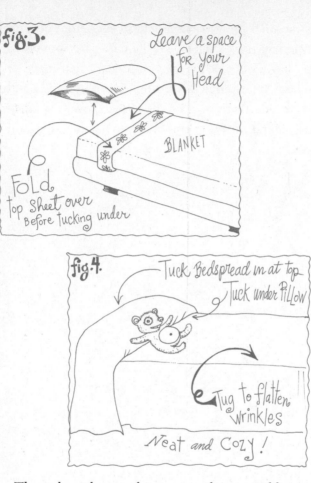

fig.3.

Leave a space for your Head

BLANKET

Fold top sheet over Before tucking under

fig.4.

Tuck Bedspread in at top

Tuck under Pillow

Tug to flatten wrinkles

Neat and Cozy!

Then place the top sheet as evenly as possible on top of the bottom sheet. You'll want the fat part of the hem to be up where your head will be. Line the top edge of the sheet with the top edge of the mattress; the sides and feet end should hang down about a foot or so. Starting with the foot of the bed, fold the top sheet under the mattress. Start in the middle and work your way to the corners, and you are ready to undertake your hospital fold. This is very difficult to describe, but since

I can't be there with you, to tell you which part to tug on and which part to fold under, I will just do my best and draw you a few diagrams, and then we can all go have a cold beverage.

Okay, so after fitting the fitted bottom sheet, and placing the top sheet on top of that, and having tucked the top sheet snugly under the mattress at the foot of the bed, tuck the corners under the mattress on the long side of the bed, making sure that the folds are flat. Pull the sheet taut as you fold in the sides. The corners should fold neatly, like origami. Add your blanket, repeating the previous step. (Also, if you don't have a fitted sheet, then simply do more fabulous origami hospital corners in all four corners of your bottom sheet, as I did when I was a child, apparently before elastic was invented.)

Fold the top sheet back over the blankets at the head of the bed, pulling the sheet back about half a foot, and tuck under the side flaps.

Slip pillowcases over the pillows.

If you have a bedspread or thin quilt, place it on the bed. Folding the top of the spread down, lay the pillows on top, then fold the spread back over them, leaving part of the spread tucked under the pillows.

Place any remaining pillows, teddy bears, or decorative inflatable party dolls over the bed covering. Now, that wasn't so difficult, was it?

A ridiculously neat bed brightens up the whole room, and by glaring contrast points out how messy the rest of the room might be. You might want to take this opportunity to look around and pick up a few things, before you have that cold beverage.

IF NOTHING ELSE: A CLEAN BATHROOM

When you are hosting friends for a dinner party, overnight, or for a weekend visit, a clean bathroom is a clear indicator that you care

This is NOT a **FUR** sceptre

IT IS A Toilet Brush.

Learn to use it well!

about your guests enough to go the extra mile. We don't all have perfect grown-up powder rooms, with pressed guest towels and fluffy bath towels. Some of us might have peeling wallpaper, or chipped plaster that needs painting, or cabinets that don't quite close properly, or a sticky hot water faucet. I know, I know. I keep meaning to get it repaired. But the point is that I keep everything clean. Especially when friends are coming over.

Some nice pictures on the wall will cover a multitude of sins. But nothing says, "Welcome! I am so glad you came to visit! Have a seat!" like a clean toilet.

Don't tell me. You have never cleaned a toilet. Or you sort of cleaned it, a few times. Well, now is the perfect time to learn how to do it properly. Before that blind date comes over for a cocktail, or your parents pop by for their first dinner in your new apartment. It's easy, remarkably satisfying, and fairly painless. Especially if you do it rather more often than you have been, up to now.

You will need: a toilet brush and some kind of cleanser. You needn't use anything too toxic, and a harsh abrasive isn't necessary unless the toilet looks as if it hasn't been scrubbed since the Mansons lived there in 1968. If you are pinching pennies, there are a host of household items that may be used to make your toilet sparkle. These will not only cost you next to nothing; their use will impress friends and dates alike that you are a gentle steward of this planet Earth. There is nothing hotter than being a gentle steward of this planet Earth.

And why not pinch pennies? You can clean your toilet (and your shower, bath, and sink) with a mixture of baking soda and vinegar. Pour some vinegar into the toilet bowl (making sure you get it as much under the rim as you can), then sprinkle some baking soda on top of it. It will start foaming, and all you'll need to do is scrub gently under the rim with your toilet brush, swishing the brush around the bowl, perhaps whistling a happy tune. If your toilet is in seriously bad shape, spray a mixture of water with a tiny amount of bleach in it, and then sprinkle the baking soda on top of that. Continue the scrubbing instructions described above, with or without the happy whistling.

A sparkling toilet, a couple of clean, folded towels within reach of the sink, a small stack of washcloths, and as a bonus, soap in a little jar, or something will spiff the place right up. You needn't have a crystal soap jar for storage; I keep extra soaps in a metal lunchbox that a friend gave me. And here's a budget-minded tip: you can get a large package of terry cloth "shop towels," found at hardware and auto-parts stores. Use them as guest towels and washcloths! Your guests will never know, and if they do figure it out, they'll think you're so cute for having thought of it first.

More Unbelievable Baking Soda Tips!

It is amazing that something that costs less than a foamy latte at your local café has so many, many uses around your house, apartment, or hovel. You've all probably heard about placing an open box of baking soda in your refrigerator to eliminate odors, and if you haven't, well honestly, it really does work. It is totally uncanny, miraculous stuff, and can be used for a really stunning variety of household needs.

1. Sprinkle directly on coffee or tea stains in cups and mugs, rub gently with sponge or washcloth and rinse. Stains will magically disappear. Seriously. It's eerie.
2. Apparently you can use it to clean greasy stove tops. I kid you not!
3. You can make it into a paste, with water, and spread it on poison oak, poison ivy, insect bites, bee stings, and itchy rashes. Weird.

Honey:
A sweetener
for your tea
AND
a hydrating Mask
for your FACE!

4. It actually kills fleas! No, really. I am freaking out. Mix equal parts table salt and baking soda and sprinkle over your carpets. Run like mad all around your carpet, or put on some bouncy music and dance on it until the soda and salt are no longer visible. Let it set overnight. In the morning, vacuum once or twice. All the adult fleas should be dead as tiny doornails, but you'll need to do the salt 'n' soda dance two more times within two weeks, to kill all the babies and eggs.

5. It stops grease fires! Amazing.

6. If you add a small handful to your dishwater, it softens hands and makes your dishes squeak. Unless you find the sound of squeaking dishes too disconcerting.

7. Okay, get this. Add a little baking soda to your facial cleanser instead of using an expensive facial scrub. Not that I don't love that Bliss exfoliating stuff, but twenty-six dollars? Hello? You can add baking soda to a paste made from instant oatmeal and water, too, for something really fancy.

8. You can use it to clean your shower curtain. Let a 1/2 cup of baking soda dissolve into, say, a gallon of water, and wipe down that moldy shower curtain. It will clean your shower-stall walls, too!

9. Use it to unclog a kitchen sink. Pour about 1/4 cup in the drain and then pour boiling water over it. Repeat if needed.

10. It is said that you can sprinkle it on oily hair if you don't have time to wash it. Hmm. Okay, if you are really in a huge hurry, sprinkle a little on your hair, comb it through, and either do a quick blow-dry, or find a nice hat to wear.

11. It is said that a little sprinkled into your laundry load will remove cigar and cigarette smells. In case you're the type who goes in for late-night clubbing.

12. This list is getting really long.
13. Use it to clean porcelain sinks and bathtubs.
14. Sprinkle it in your shoes to absorb moisture and get rid of that horrible stink.
15. Sprinkle it in your bathwater to relieve irritated or itchy skin.
16. Sprinkle into your stinky garbage can! Or, maybe you could just empty your garbage.
17. It allegedly cleans crayon off floors and such. Just in case you are still taken to scribbling on the walls and floors, or you have guests who engage in that kind of behavior.
18. Are you totally astounded at this stuff? No, really, baking soda. It is just so cool.
19. Okay, mix a little baking soda and vinegar just to watch it fizz. Whoa. Is that wild, or what? Now go clean something.
20. Yes, it even works on vomit. So the next time that friend of a friend blows chunks on your bathroom rug, give him a handful of paper towels and a box of baking soda. Tell him to remove all solid matter first; then have him dump a load of baking soda onto the offending area. Watch as it magically wicks the liquid up out of the carpet! Ew! Okay, don't watch. Then have him pick up the wet clumps, and vacuum the rest. Then put him to bed on your sofa, with a glass of water and two aspirin. With, perhaps, a bucket and a towel nearby.

If all that weren't enough (and there's more, I omitted mention of baking soda's ant deterrent capabilities! Or how it can be used as a laundry softener, hair and age-spot lightener, toothpaste, and baby powder!), you can use baking soda as a leavening agent in, yes, *baking*. It may be used to make banana bread, and pancakes, and so many other delicious baked goods. And it will make your hair curl, and can bring about world peace! That last part may not be entirely true. But baking soda *can* make you richer, because of all the money you won't be spending on all those expensive cleaning products.

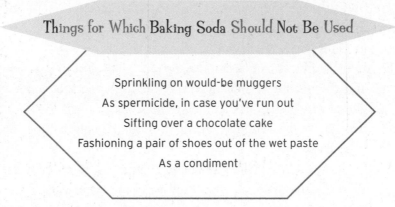

Things for Which Baking Soda Should Not Be Used

Sprinkling on would-be muggers
As spermicide, in case you've run out
Sifting over a chocolate cake
Fashioning a pair of shoes out of the wet paste
As a condiment

GETTING A LIPSTICK STAIN OUT OF YOUR SHIRT

If you are unable to get your shirt immediately into the laundry, blot the stain with water to keep it from setting. Use a small amount of water so the stain does not bleed. Do not frantically rub the lipstick stain, or it will smear, which will look much, much worse.

If the item is washable, cover the stain with some of your magic baking soda and moisten it with a damp sponge or brush. Let it sit for five minutes.

Next, apply prewash stain remover to the lipstick and allow it to soak according to the instructions. If the stain is set in or heavy, allow the stain remover to soak in overnight. If you don't have any prewash stain remover, use some dishwashing soap.

Wash the item according to the instructions on the label. Repeat if the stain remains.

Do not put your shirt in the dryer if a trace of the stain remains, because heat will set the stain. Hang it out in a sunny spot, or on your shower head (so the shower will catch any water drips), or laid out over a towel. If all else fails, you can bring the garment to a professional dry cleaner.

If the item is dry-clean only, bring it to a professional dry cleaner, and let them know that you have a lipstick stain. Ignore possible smirking.

If you don't have baking soda in your cupboard, go get some! Have we learned nothing from my comprehensive treatise on baking soda? If you foolishly have not stocked up on baking soda, here is a tip I found on the Internet: spray some hairspray on the lipstick and wait until it dries completely. Then wash the offending garment. It is apparently "foolproof." Or next time you're making out with your red-lipsticked temptress, wear a black t-shirt, and alleviate the whole problem.

A red wine spill is best lifted with a dousing of club soda, or a paste of baking soda and water, or, strangely enough, a splash of white wine.

To remove spaghetti sauce, you can try cold water or club soda. If that doesn't work, you might have to resort to a prewash stain remover.

For oil, butter, and other greasy spills, shake some baby powder on the stain, letting the powder suck up the grease before shaking off the powder. There is a product out there called Goo Gone, which you might want to keep on hand if you are prone to spilling an immoderate amount of greasy stuff down your front throughout the day, and you really would rather have that goo be gone. It will evidently clean up any kind of stain.

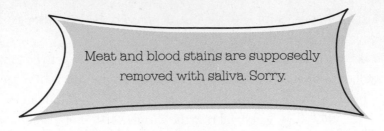

Meat and blood stains are supposedly removed with saliva. Sorry.

EVENT CLEANING

Perhaps you sit in the shadows, night after night, hoping to surreptitiously observe and document the activities of your elusive housekeeping elves and cleaning fairies. You have found their droppings, and you've attempted to put them under surveillance for months. But they are wily creatures, and apparently quickly abandon their cleaning-up duties as soon as they realize they're being watched.

Or possibly you are conducting an experiment to see how long a person can live in a house or apartment without cleaning it. How big, exactly, do those dust bunnies grow? Really big, or enormous? Do the dust bunnies tend to collect more under the bed, under the sofa, in the corners of every room, or all of the above? Are dust bunnies actually shaped like real bunnies? Is there a possible connection between your occasional fits of sneezing and the extra dust? Who named them "dust bunnies" anyway? Did you know that an extra layer of grease on a stove top actually traps flies and moths? And isn't it amazing how a fairly thick film of something that looks like moss appears to be growing around the water line of your toilet? What exactly is the life cycle of maggots, and how did they get into my bathroom drain?

The world may be breathlessly anticipating the results of your exhaustive study, but you have just discovered that some friends are dropping by your place tonight. Or you have a date you might want to bring back after a movie. Or your grandmother is coming for dinner. Someone may need to use the bathroom.

When I have let my house go a little too long between cleanings, I find I am instantly invigorated by the idea that within hours, friends and/or family will be sitting in my bathroom looking closely at their immediate surroundings for what could be more than a few minutes. Chances are they'll be checking out the inside of the medicine chest too, because, come on, everyone does.

Your guests might find themselves eating off a plate at your kitchen table, or possibly sitting on your sofa. You really don't want anyone to leave your apartment by ambulance, nor would it be conducive to a romantic evening to have those crusty gym socks you were looking for turn up pecking out from under a sofa cushion.

You don't have time to call in the hazmat team for a thorough hot steam and fumigation, and you cannot imagine tackling the piles that have grown exponentially on your dining table. Looking at the kitchen just sends you on a crying jag.

Snap out of it! You're a grown-up now. You are about to laugh in the face of disaster. Your habitat is the disaster, and you are going to have an event. So this is how to undertake a fairly speedy but thorough "event cleaning."

First, tackle the piles of magazines and papers that are piled on the table where presumably everyone will be eating and/or drinking. Make a stack (or stacks) out of the magazines. Then gather and make a neat pile out of the papers, bills, unpaid parking tickets, and notes from your mother asking why you never call.

If you read a newspaper, I already love you more than you can know. If your newspaper is from two Sundays ago, is covered in pizza stains, and is scattered all over the table, perhaps you're finished with the news and can place it in the recycle bin. (If you don't have a recycle bin, start one immediately. Didn't I already mention that sensitive stewards of the Earth are hopelessly attractive?)

Place your magazine stacks on a free surface such as a side table, with the most interesting magazines on top. If you have no side table, put the stack on a chair that won't be needed, possibly that broken one that no one can sit in anyway. If you have no free surfaces of any kind, place the magazines on the floor, against a wall in a neat stack that says, "I meant to put these magazines on the floor. I'm oversubscribed. But only because I am such a voracious information junkie. I stack books on the floor, too. I am just that kind of fascinating, slightly scattered intellectual."

Next, move on to the bathroom. Now you've got something bubbling on the stove, and you still haven't changed your clothes. People are due in forty-five minutes, unless they're late, which you're sort of hoping they will be. But the bathroom must be tackled. There is *stuff* on the porcelain rim of the toilet when you lift up the seat, and something that seems vaguely gooey around the base of the sink faucets. How did it get there? It looks like something a slug might excrete. Around the base of the faucets. That is totally disgusting. Also, the sink seems to be lined with a crust of dried toothpaste. But okay! We can slap this puppy into shape in no time.

You really will have to see to the bathroom in a big way when you have more time, but in the interim, find a sponge, one that is old and has served its purpose in the world, because you'll be throwing it out afterward. Grab a wad of paper towels while you're at it. Also, grab any kind of liquid soap product, which will do in a pinch if you don't have any scrubby stuff or a jar of Mrs. Bubbles Happy Crapper. Okay, there is no such cleaning product, but there should be.

Finally, unless I remember something else that you'll need, grab an empty grocery bag or garbage bag. You will be bringing it from room to room to dispose of trash and other rubbish you want to get rid of in a hurry. But first, to the bathroom.

Quick, drip a little soap into the sink and scrub it down thoroughly with a wet sponge until it's squeaky. You don't want to use a lot of soap. In this instance you are using hot water and elbow grease, which means you are making up in muscle and natural resources what you lack in the cleaning product department. When the sink has been cleaned, fill it up with hot water and a little more soap. Splash down the faucets and use the sponge to wipe down the sink area. Wipe down the doorknobs and any windowsills, ledges, or picture frames that can be scrutinized from the toilet or sink area. Wipe down the top and *outside* of the toilet.

Drain the sink and wipe it out with some paper towels. Take a paper towel and shine up the faucets, the mirror, and around the sink. With a few of the hot-water-dampened paper towels, wipe down the toilet seat. The actual seat part, where people sit. Wipe down the inside of the top of the toilet lid. Then gingerly lift the toilet seat and take a brush to the new life forms that are lining the bowl (use baking soda and vinegar, or a little soap). Then take one of your paper towels and wipe up all visible, um, gunk on the rim and environs. You are done with that paper towel. Throw it away immediately in the receptacle you have brought with you, into which you will also dump your overflowing bathroom trash.

Take the rest of your paper towels and wipe down any parts of the floor that seem particularly egregious, taking special pains to mop up the furry balls of hair that are lurking in the corners. Now look around, quickly, and make sure that anything that should be shiny is polished, and that there are no gobs of anything unusual peeking out from any corners.

If you have bathroom rugs, now would be a good time to give them

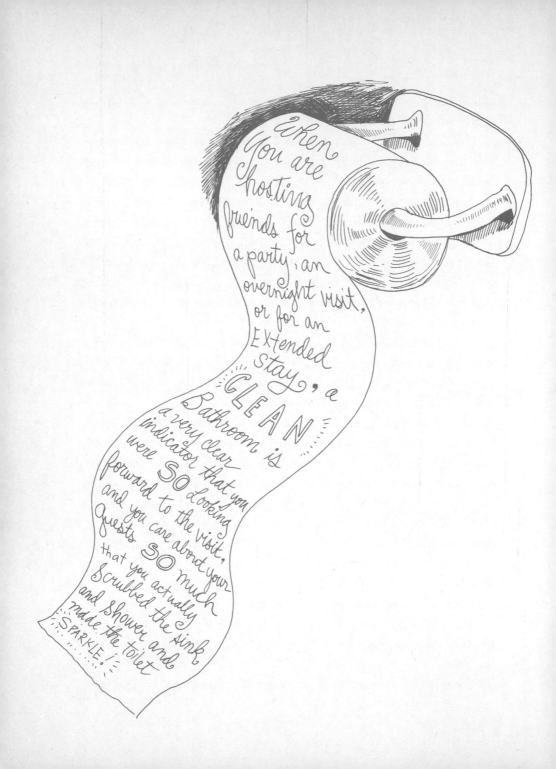

When you are hosting friends for a party, an overnight visit, or for an EXtended stay, a CLEAN Bathroom is a very clear indicator that you were SO looking forward to the visit, and you care about your guests SO much that you actually scrubbed the sink and shower and made the toilet SPARKLE!

a good shake, outside. If they are really cruddy, fold them up neatly and place them out of sight somewhere. The bathroom might look cleaner without them. For a final touch, you might light a scented votive candle or put a small vase of flowers by the sink. If you have no flowers, use some rosemary from your neighbor's yard (mind the vicious doggie!) or place a few stalks of the basil that you're using for dinner into a jar, or wineglass. Remind yourself to start a small herb garden and to plant some nasturtiums, which grow like weeds, and can be used for dainty bathroom flower arrangements, *and* can be tossed in a salad and eaten! (Ahem, but not the ones from the bathroom, please.)

Okay, where were we? Now you are sweating, and you still haven't put on your party clothes. Why are you running so late? We'll talk about punctuality a little later. In the meantime, let's move onto the living room, or the nook where your sofa or some loose arrangement of chairs sits waiting for your guests to plop their behinds. If they are covered with magazines, papers, and such, please refer to the spot several paragraphs back where I describe how to clean the table on which you dine. Using the same technique, quickly divest yourself of all similar piles on your sofa. Plump the pillows, if any, and, as in the case of my sofa, reposition the lovely shawl you have draped artfully so as to cover the big rip in the upholstery.

Grab your broom. (You will need a broom and a dustpan. Did I mention that? Make sure you have one of each on hand. They're very archaic looking and basic, but amazingly useful, sort of like aspirin.) Now do a quick sweep around all seating and dining areas.

Before you head into your room to throw on some less sweaty clothing and comb your hair, splash water on your face and/or apply a swathe of red lipstick, walk through your front door and see if there is anything glaringly unwelcoming there to greet you upon entering. And don't worry about the kitchen. Presumably you've been preparing food in there, and possibly have something simmering on the stove. You'll be heading back in there as your guests arrive, so try to clean as you go. Whatever mess was in there before will be masked, we hope, by whatever mess you're making for your guests.

If there are still piles of things scattered around the living room, your bed, or anywhere else people might congregate, pile it all into your closet or under the bed. I know it's a cliché. But it will have the desired effect, at least temporarily. And the best thing is, it will force you to have a real cleanup at a more convenient time.

Sometimes event cleaning is the only cleaning that gets done around my house. But I look at that as yet another wonderful reason to have friends over more often. Everyone benefits. Eventually you will need to clean less superficially and a little more thoroughly than you do for an event, but the event cleaning will tide you over until some free Saturday when you can really roll up your sleeves and get elbow deep into the muck.

If you've put out a few snacks and beverages and are a welcoming host or hostess, you will no doubt have a lovely party and no one will notice if your house isn't perfect. And who wants a perfect house? A perfect house is a myth as attainable as a unicorn-fur smoking jacket, and about as necessary. But a comfortable house, a cozy apartment, a place where people feel at ease and at home—a place filled with friends—is the most perfect house of all.

WHAT IS THAT HORRIBLE MOLDY SMELL?

Will you please not leave your sponge in the sink? It is totally annoying and disgusting. You aren't the only one who does it, older people who should know better do it, but you have to stop. If you leave your sponge in the sink, every time the water runs or you dump something down the drain, your sponge just stays all wet, growing all kinds of bacteria. Then it starts giving off that dank, moldy smell. And then you wash your dishes with it! And then you wipe your counter and wash some cup you just drank out of with it! You may have just cleaned up that spill on the floor with it, before washing the glass that I am about to drink out of. Ew! Seriously, ew.

Try this, instead. After using your sponge for washing up, rinse it out and squeeze as much water as you can out of the sponge. Set your sponge up somewhere, out of sink, next to the sink, maybe, or in its own special sponge rack. Your sponge will last a lot longer, first of all. Second of all, you need to use a separate sponge for your countertops and stove spills, so you won't be spreading E. coli and plague onto your coffee cups every time you wash them. And you'll need a third sponge for your floor spills. Get different colors! Make your kitchen sink area a fun place to be.

If your sponge is starting to get "that smell," you can prolong the life of it (for a little while, anyway) by putting it in a bowl of water to which you have added about a teaspoon of bleach. Or you can boil it in water for five minutes.

When my dish sponge starts to get a little past its prime, I give it a new life as the countertop sponge. When the countertop sponge starts looking a little tired, it will be recycled into a floor sponge. And it will be so grateful for the new job, knowing that it has become a part of the great Circle of Life for sponges: beginning life as a dish sponge, and ending it as a floor sponge.

When your sponge has become totally repulsive, throw it away; or boil it again and cut it into festive shapes to use as sponge stamps on all your correspondence.

GET YOUR FASHION AND HOME DECORATING
TIPS FROM THE MOVIES!

Perhaps you've seen those catalogues that hawk the home-furnishing industry's version of a cardigan sweater and a pair of chinos. Safe, tasteful, not inexpensive, but not completely out of reach, it is totally grown-up furniture and decor. But is it you? Maybe you're not really sure exactly what "you" is, yet. But you have a tiny inkling that "you" is not that handsome wood-veneered French country sideboard, or the cute bistro chalkboard with the rooster on it, or that knotty-pine kitchen table. The gleaming sleigh bed is pretty, but it just seems too solid, or something, and it is entirely lacking in fun.

A living space that has a sense of humor is a fun living space, and can cost far less to assemble than buying an entire suite of furniture from a home-décor showroom. So have fun when you're putting together your place. Mix flea-market finds with the occasional new piece. See what you can scrounge from your family—they might be ready to toss something out that could be useful, as well as sentimentally valuable to you. And if you're looking for inspiration, there are movies out there that are enormously inspirational to the incipient home decorator. They're not all great movies, but chock-full of some of the most kicky, over-the-top, and delightful decorating ideas. The list, to which you may of course add your own selections, includes the following:

* Any one of the original James Bond films, especially *Dr. No*, where Bond ends up in Jamaica, shaking his martinis in a totally hip Colonial-Caribbean cabana-motel room. Check out those Danish modern chairs!
* Any Douglas Sirk movie, in fabulous Technicolor, especially

All This and Heaven Too. Feel the repression. And look at those drapes!

✳ *Flower Drum Song* is a must-see, if only for the visual candy that is Sammy Fong's swingin' bachelor pad.

✳ *What a Way to Go*, with Shirley MacLaine. Sheer inspiration. Go for the fashion and decorating tips, stay for the Gene Kelly soft shoe, Paul Newman's monkey, and the half-lidded smirks of Robert (grrrrowl) Mitchum. (Big pothead, by the way. Get some tips on how cool a single human can be.) Plus, Shirley MacLaine with pink hair! No more need be said.

✳ *A New Kind of Love*, with Paul Newman and Joanne Woodward. New York. Paris. Paul and Joanne. Don't go looking for the PC, you will not find it. It's a new kind of terrible, really, in spite of Paul and Joanne. Instead, enjoy the goofy tongue-in-cheekiness, the cool room dividers, and built-in prehistoric TV sets, the hanging lamps that threaten to decapitate, and the coolest rust-orange sofa ever. Bullet bras! Great hats! Stunning 1960s fashion models! Horribly corny Maurice Chevalier cameo!

✳ *Attack of the Mushroom People* is all about bad dubbing and 1960s Japanese western-style fashions. Along these same lines, *Godzilla vs. Mothra* must be seen for the tiny singing fairy twins sporting matching pink pillbox hats. Smart!

✳ *A Shot in the Dark* and the other Pink Panther movies are not only stylish, they are really funny. If you haven't seen Peter Sellers in anything before, immediately rush out and rent these. Make lots of popcorn. For you and your Minky.

✳ According to my friend Henry, you must see *A Clockwork Orange*, so you can check out the cat lady's cool décor, with the "rocking lingam sculpture." Before she gets killed by the droogies.

✳ Henry also likes the moon space station where the Russians meet with the American scientist in *2001: A Space Odyssey*.

✳ *Sabrina*, the original version, of course—for the chauffeur's above-the-garage suite. Cuh-lassay.

✳ The Fab Four's insanely hip adjacent flats with the matching doors, which reveal the fabulous pad inside, in the Beatles movie *Help!* Pay close attention to John's groovy sunken bed or rumpus area. I want one, too!

In Case You Didn't Get the Memo

IN THE WORKPLACE

So you have a new job. Maybe you finally got the dream job of a lifetime, or maybe you just found something that will pay the bills and keep a roof over your head. It's the job you've been hoping for all your young life, or it's just a job. It'll do until something better comes along. Either way, you need to commit to this job. You've accepted the job, and as long as you're going to be doing this job, you might as well do it capably.

If there is something you don't know how to do on this job, learn how to do it, and do it to the best of your ability. Do it with panache. Do it with grace and good cheer. Whether you are slinging hash, waiting tables, driving a cab, or working in the upper echelons of a venerated financial institution, publishing house, or law firm, you must do your job as if you mean it, and like it, and have something unique to bring to it. You *do* have something unique to bring to the job. You!

Okay, fine, the job sucks. But you're going to be there anyway, so you might as well take some pride in what you're doing. Be interested in what you do, instead of thinking about how you're going to party over the weekend. This attitude will serve you well in all places of employment, as well as later on in life, when you realize you have a wealth of knowledge gleaned from all the various and interesting jobs you've had.

Let's say you're starting a new job in some office. You might want to think about the impression you will be making in those first delicate weeks. You might want to think about how you'll present yourself, and how you'll go about making yourself a valuable and necessary part of your new place of employment. Or you might just be utterly clueless, and have to learn through trial and error, just like so many before you.

A NOTE TO THE NEW GUY

Listen, you just started three days ago, and no one wants to tell you this, but somebody has to: quit sidling up to our cubicles and getting all chummy with us. We don't know you. We might have wanted to get to know you, but within an hour of your arrival you started swaggering around like you've had this job for fifteen years and you're everybody's best buddy. No, you giant ass, *I've* been working here for fifteen years. You are the new guy. It is just icky the way you're all relaxed. I mean, relaxed is good, but you're all, like, lounge-lizardy relaxed.

I know, it's sort of a casual place, and you see people joking around and being sociable, and pretty cozy with one another, and generally behaving as if they have all been living together in a commune for years. *This is not an invitation for you to approach the executive secretary in the adjoining cubicle and give her a neck massage.* And we don't want to hear you pipe in with your hilariously raunchy joke just because you overheard Don in HR stop by with his stupid joke of the day. We hate

Don in HR and his stupid joke of the day. You would know that if you just shut up and kept your ears open. Now, don't go and start hating Don in HR, either; *we* are allowed to hate Don in HR. You don't get to hate him yet, because you haven't been here long enough to hate anybody.

Until you have worked at this job for many more months, and have been invited to socialize with your coworkers, you must not behave as if you are a long-standing member of our happy family. You are not allowed to do that yet. You are not allowed to make amusing remarks about Heather's bad hair, just because you heard others do it. Don't assume that you are "one of the gang" until you have been invited to be "one of the gang." This could take years.

Also, we really don't want to hear that you are a martial arts master, or that you have "healing hands," or that your father was required to purchase a hundred-million-dollar insurance policy on you because he is, well, kind of a Big Oil CEO, and, of course, kidnapping is a problem. Even if it's true.

Do not feel the need to share every bit of information about yourself and your life, especially within the first hour of meeting your coworkers. And if you're "slumming," your older coworkers may not want to hear that you bought your first house at nineteen, and about how "Paris" was at the "wrap" party you attended the previous evening. That goes double if you are the boss's nephew. Are you the boss's nephew? Because that is just pathetic. Listen, we want to be nice. But you have got to learn the lay of the land a little. Just keep the ol' piehole in a relaxed, closed position, and you'll be fine. Now go do something useful.

A QUICK ASIDE TO MISS UNDERGROUND INDIE GIRL

Not to be picky, but is that pierced lip a must-have fashion statement for the office? Not that I don't adore interesting fashion statements, but did you wear it for your job interview? If you did, and you got the job, then you must be delighted to be working in such a relaxed and forgiving environment. If you didn't, perhaps you shouldn't spring it on everyone in the office right away. In fact, it might be a good idea to keep the whole lip, eyebrow, belly-button, and nose piercings under wraps for the time being, along with the large tribal tattoo that adorns your upper back. I'm just saying. I'm all for self-expression, but it's just one of those etiquette things, making sure those around you are comfortable. If it would make your boss uncomfortable to look at the steel ring that is stuck through your eyebrow and connected by a chain to your nose, then you might want to wait a little while before fluffing that particular bit of your plumage. Perhaps the company holiday party would be a good time to whip out the face jewelry. After your boss has had several glasses of rum punch.

A BRIEF MEMO TO BRITTANY

If you are a new, young, eye-catching female, you may find that you're getting some attention from Chip in accounts, or Rob in legal affairs, or even the big guy upstairs. Do not let your head get turned by the sleazebag down the hall, or even the one in the head office. He may be full of pretty compliments, he may shower you with attention, or he may even ask for a date, which is entirely inappropriate. If—after months of bonding, friendship, and a splotch of frisson—you think you have found true love and he professes to have found same, tell him that true love lasts the ages, and will certainly last your tenure at this job. If a flame still burns after a year of bad office coffee, then it will certainly last for an eternity. If you decide that this is the job you want for the rest of your life and neither one of you has any intention of moving on to other places of employment, well, then you have a little dilemma. After a year or two of mutual longing and admiration, you can decide, as two adults, how to proceed. But don't fall for the office flirt your first week on the job, or it will be painful and possibly embarrassing to go to the office.

Also, do I have to say this? I don't want to hear the intimate details of your sex life, either, even if we have been working side by side for a whole week. I don't know how I possibly could have given you the impression that I was keenly interested in minutiae about the sexual encounter you and your date had in an unusual public location. And I hate to be a big wet blanket, but I really wish you wouldn't share your fondest hopes for another three-way.

Unless you work in the cubicle next to a blood relative or *extremely* close friend, avoid sharing detailed descriptions of the physical attributes of your most recent date, or asking your colleague to check your "mysterious back cancer," which will be instantly recognizable as rug burns from having at it on your living-room carpet. There are some images we don't necessarily want to have seared into our brain.

Yes, you are very, very attractive! Now, please get to work.

A QUICK COMMUNIQUÉ TO OUR NEW FASHIONISTA

I know you paid two hundred dollars for those jeans, but they have a giant rip in the butt! Really! Oh my God, it's huge! Did you know that?

Or did you actually pay extra for that rip? I know you probably think it was so totally worth it, but that particular stretch of skin that is peeking through the rip is not the area code of skin that you really want to be showing your boss and coworkers.

You need to steer clear of showing body parts that are not work-related body parts. Because unless your place of employment is one where ripped jeans, tight baby-tees, and five inches of mesh skirt are encouraged in its employees, you are probably better off saving your civvies for the weekends and after-hours. Most of us manage to avoid the scourge of uncomfortably overheated abdomens without resorting to midriff tops, oddly enough. Showing up in a cellophane bathing suit might make for some entertaining watercooler chat among your coworkers, but you might not be taken as seriously in the workplace as you hope to be.

Also, you know how your thong panties show at the top of your jeans? Isn't that over yet as a "look"? Because it just makes no sense, and may compel me to give you a wedgie.

YOU THERE, WITH THE BIG SHINY APPLE ON YOUR DESK

I just wanted to let you know that we all see you frantically and beaverishly sidling up to the boss to compliment her scarf, or laugh heartily at her wretched forays into humor, or offer to get his coffee with the special fake sweetener that he likes. You keep an extra box of that fake sweetener in your cubicle, so that you'll always be there to save the day when the office kitchen runs out. Yay for you!

We notice that you pay six hundred dollars for a haircut—*a haircut*—plus a tip, just to ensure forty-five minutes of insults and humiliation at the hands of the hairdresser, because you think going to the same salon as your boss will earn you some Brownie points or something. You are spending your free weekends learning *golf*, you craven crawler, so you can talk *golf* with your boss in hopes of getting an invitation to the links. And you step up your toadying as we draw closer to the holidays, hoping your sycophancy will be rewarded, hoping a few stray pieces of eight will be in your bonus envelope in response to all your hard, hard work and obsequiousness. You are the Eddie Haskell of the office, and we are all getting tense from cringing so much. Please, grow a soul, and maybe a backbone, on your next long weekend, you fawning bootlicker.

YOUR NEW JOB, IN A PERFECT WORLD

Ideally, your first day of work would unfold something like this:

Since you are new to this job, you will want to give yourself an extra bit of time to get there, so that you arrive early. Know where you're going. This might entail doing a test drive over to the new office a few days before the job starts, or taking the bus or subway to the area, just to see how long your commute might be, unless you are very familiar with getting to that part of town. On the first day of your new job, you will want to give yourself plenty of extra time for traffic jams, late buses, and parking.

Enter your new place of employment relaxed from having left early and not rushing to work. Cheerfully greet your boss, or your boss's secretary, or whomever it is you are supposed to check in with. Instead of standing around looking vague and helpless, ask where the supply closet is located. Hie yourself immediately to the supply room, and avail yourself of its contents. Bring back whatever it is you need to have on your desk: pencils, pens, notepads, Post-Its. It might have been a good idea for you to bring your own coffee cup for coffee breaks; proceed to write BRING COFFEE CUP on a fresh Post-It.

If you are unsure of what to do next, ask for your assignments. Ask as many questions as you need to ask. Important caveat: know when to stop asking questions. If your coworkers are forced to answer questions all day long, they will soon tire of it, and possibly, you. Use some of that initiative I know you have. Keep your eyes peeled and use your keen deduction skills to figure out where they're hiding the printer paper, and how to use the phone.

Presumably, you will have been briefed on the basic office machinery, but if you don't know how to use the copier or fax machine, ask someone. But try not to ask your boss.

Do your job, impeccably and good-naturedly. Keep your eyes and ears open before you plunge into the cauldron of office politics.

When five o'clock rolls around, or six, or whenever your workday is finished, don't bolt out of there as if you've been held against your will for eight hours. When your day is done, it's always a good idea to check in with your boss, perhaps asking if there's anything else that needs to be done before you leave. If you establish yourself as a person who is on time, takes direction graciously, works cheerfully, and is always eager to help, you will be met with understanding and forgiveness, should you happen to be tardy one day, or should you need to call in sick.

Avoid calling in sick on too many Mondays because of excessive weekend revelry. It will become annoying to your boss and coworkers, and will wreak havoc on your skin tone.

A NOTE TO THE ART DOGS

Even if you have decided to devote your life to the arts, and you don't punch a time card or commute to a cubicle every day, you still need to be on time for appointments, and dressed as if you didn't crawl out of a cardboard box. When you are a famous artist you may dress as if you crawled out of a cardboard box, if it pleases you. But in the meantime, if you want to be taken seriously, you should attempt to project the same kind of professionalism as a more conventionally employed worker.

Being the proud possessor of an enormous amount of dazzling talent doesn't give you special dispensation to drink yourself stupid and behave rudely. There are a great many artistic types out there, many of them with an enormous amount of dazzling talent *and* a nice dollop of humility and good manners.

THE WORKING LIFE

If you think you have found your dream job, and you want this job more than anything in the world, and for some inexplicable reason you are not hired for this job, do not despair. A better opportunity will come along immediately. It just will. It always does. Really. You are allowed a day or two of wallowing in your pain, but then slap yourself around a little and get back out there. Look deep into yourself, and try to figure out if there was something you could have done differently in your job interview. If you really don't understand why you were passed over for the job, if there seems to be no earthly reason why they wouldn't have chosen you, the reason probably lies entirely out of your control, and you just have to trust that you did the best you could. It is not the end of the world. If you are in your twenties, this is not the end of your working life.

There are two kinds of people in their twenties. Okay, maybe there are more, but for the sake of conversation, let's just say there are those who know what they want to be when they grow up, and those who have no bleeding clue and are beginning to panic. The panic starts setting in as they get closer to thirty, the year that most people think of as real, for sure, we-are-so-not-kidding-this-time adulthood. It is, like, *old* adulthood. There is no hiding behind the cute "I'm in my twenties!" thing anymore. It's time for big boy pants, and possibly, an actual *career*.

You may be paralyzed with the fear of failure. You may fear venturing outside the expectations you—and possibly your parents—have for yourself. You may think that you are a loser because you are not on any career track, or you are not romantically linked with anyone. You have made seemingly no commitments to anything but the gym, your drinking schedule, and your busy social life. You may think you are postponing the onset of your adult life by putting off any real commitment for as long as possible. But the fact is, you *will* be forty years old one day, and you will not believe how quickly that day will be upon you. It is absolutely startling. So, since we've established that you're going to be forty anyway, you might as well do *something* with yourself.

Okay, here's a good, old-fashioned inspirational story. A friend of mine who made quite a decent living acting in television commercials and soap operas decided, at the age of thirty-six, that she didn't want to be a struggling actor twenty years on. She wanted to get her PhD in psychology.

This is a person who had always been described as "so pretty!"—which is another way of saying, "Thank goodness you are so pretty, because you are really not very smart and if you're lucky you'll marry well." But here she was, at the age of thirty-six, thinking she was a dumb, pretty person, having never attended a *day of college*, deciding that she wanted a PhD in psychology.

She figured it would take her nine years, but reasoned that she was going to be forty-five anyway, so she might as well have a PhD when she got there. She started at the local community college, transferred to UCLA, wrote a bunch of papers, blah blah blah, until she got her master's degree. Then she got an internship, wrote a thesis on something or other, and received her PhD. And we had a big party. Now she makes everyone call her "doctor," which would be insufferable, except that she really is a doctor and helps crazy people and whatnot. So the thing is, you really *can* do whatever you set your mind to do. My friend had previously done nothing with her life but hawk Jif peanut butter on TV and say "one moment please" as the swarthy guy's secretary on *The Young and the Restless*. And her spelling is terrible! If she could do it, anyone can.

I have another friend who is a very successful voice-over guy. He has scads of money and steady work. For years he has done fake sportscaster voices for television shows and movies; he's really good at it. The weird thing is, all this time he secretly longed to be a real baseball announcer, and suddenly last year he decided to see if he could do it. So here's a successful guy who doesn't really need another job, but in his off hours he drives an hour or more to a tiny minor-league ballpark where he interns as a baseball color announcer. He does tons of research, drives a ridiculous distance, and works odd hours for no money so that older, more experienced announcers can lord it over him and make him work like a young rookie announcer. He is working his butt off, but is following his passion. And he loves it, and it turns out he is just as good at being a real baseball announcer.

So learn how to do something that you love. If you have no passion for anything right now, work on developing a passion, or several passions. That way you'll have something to fall back on when your strict schedule of working out, partying, and drinking starts getting a little old.

GET A CRAPPY JOB!

Getting a crappy job is a must-do, if you want to grow up to be an interesting, well-rounded individual. You will learn skills that, much to your surprise, will come in really handy years later. You will probably learn how to deal with scary managers and unusual and/or difficult working conditions. You will undoubtedly come away from any crappy job with enough stories to regale your friends and dates for years to come. All this, and they'll pay you, too! They actually won't pay you much, usually, if it's a genuinely crappy job. But a mere pile of money pales in comparison with the many priceless rewards that a crappy job can bring. You will be able to break the ice at parties and keep friends and family entertained with tales of your crappy job. If you have a crappy job *and* a crazy boss, you are one lucky stiff. Enjoy! Or, try to enjoy. I know it's hard to imagine when you are in the middle of the crappy job that it could ever make you happy. But one day, you will look back on your crappy job years and be thrilled you had those crappy jobs.

And just as every director should be required to take acting classes, everyone in the world who patronizes restaurants on a fairly regular basis should, at least once in their lives, wait tables. You need to know exactly how much work is involved in waiting tables before you blithely order your waitperson about, or even consider leaving a stingy tip.

Believe it or not, your future employers actually look at your crappy job history as a good thing, at least the really interesting ones do. Holding down a number of crappy jobs shows your resourcefulness and ability to deal with a variety of situations. It indicates that you are not saddled with an overweening sense of self-importance. It implies an intrepid spirit and a blessed lack of hubris. These are all traits that are sought after by the smartest employers. These are also traits that might make you your own employer. All hail the crappy job!

YOUR RÉSUMÉ: DID YOU REALLY CLIMB EVEREST?

Okay, this just seems so obvious that I shouldn't even have to mention it, but honestly, fudging your résumé, adding little bits of slightly exaggerated information to your past work history, inflating your job experience, and embellishing your curriculum vitae is just a really, really bad idea. List a whole batch of mad skills that you don't exactly possess, or educational degrees that you didn't exactly earn, and you are sure to be found out, as usually happens with any lie. Aside from certain U.S. presidents, most bosses are familiar with "The Google" and use it on a regular basis. Lying about things in general is not a good way to make your way through life, because you have to remember which lies you told to whom, and it gets very messy and complicated. Lying on your résumé will be found out, and will only make you an object of derision.

Most bosses, just like most people, appreciate honesty. If you are eager, bright, and willing to learn, it will go much further than a long list of make-em-ups passing for a résumé.

"Curriculum vitae" is Latin for "life story," by the way. You are twentysomething. No one expects you to have an extensive life history. They just want you to have a real one.

YOUR WACKY BOSS!

You like work, you really do. You are a loyal worker bee, but something is not quite right. Your boss doesn't seem to like you—at least, on some days. Other days your boss thinks you're great, but you're just not sure. Most of the time you walk around on eggshells because you have no idea whether today is the day he'll reach down your throat, pull your intestines out, and eat them, or if it's the day he takes everyone out for ice cream and cotton candy. Who can keep track?

Is it you? Maybe it's you. It's probably you. What is wrong with you? Okay, just so you don't worry yourself sick thinking it's you, you should know that it might not be you. You may just have a crazy boss!

Many of us have worked for crazy bosses at one time or another. But when you're in your twenties and fairly new to the workplace, it may seem as if that's the way all bosses are, that's just how it's supposed to be on the job, and you better get used to it. Your job is fun, most of the time, and most of the time your boss is a reasonable human being. "He's just a little eccentric, that's all," you think. "She's just a little moody," you tell yourself, after undergoing yet another public humiliation.

Not all bosses are prone to tantrums and bullying; some are just plain weird. And it's possible for even the best, most even-tempered boss to go wacko at least once. But if you are new to the workplace and it feels as if your job has turned into a roller coaster ride of hormones, mood swings, and possible mental imbalance, it might be helpful to have a little guide, a little crib sheet, to help you more easily spot the really unhinged boss. It may not make your job easier, knowing your boss is a walking piñata of sheer, unbridled insanity, but at least you won't go into work thinking it's all your fault, which should make your step up the ladder just a little bit lighter.

After six months, your boss still can't remember your name, and insists on calling you David. "Why do I wanna call you David?" You have no idea. Your name is not David, and there are no other Davids in the office.

> You think: I haven't made an impression of any kind on my boss. I should try harder, somehow.

> Probable reality: Your boss is totally uninvolved in his job, and is probably moving on to another job. Or, possibly, a retirement home.

Your gay boss grabs your butt for the second time in two weeks.

> You think: When he did it the first time, I must not have made it clear enough that I'm not gay. I must be acting gay in some way. Maybe it's my pants.

> Probable reality: No, he just forgot that he grabbed your butt two weeks ago. He does it to everybody. But those *are* nice pants.

Your boss offers conversation to you and other underlings in the form of "tinkle breaks," trips to the ladies' bathroom where deep conversations are held while peeing.

> You think: My boss wants to be bestest pals with me. She must really want me to be her special confidante! Even thought it's kind of weird to pee and talk.

> Probable reality: Your boss cannot stand to be alone for two minutes, because it reminds her that she is only a hu-

man, and not a boss. She must keep underlings with her at all times to remind herself that she really is the big cheese.

Your boss seems so distracted by his obsessive sock shopping that he is unable to make decisions, and you must make decisions for him.

> **You think:** My boss is really detached, and prefers argyle socks to making decisions.

> **Probable reality:** Your boss doesn't like to make any decisions that might hang him. He'd rather someone else take the fall for a bad decision, while he gets the credit for the good ones. Plus, he really does have a thing for argyle socks.

Your boss goes wacko on everyone else except you.

> **You think:** It's my job to apologize for his behavior and clean up the mess he left behind.

> **Probable reality:** He has burned so many bridges that he has no one else to clean up his messes. Sucker.

Your boss calls late at night to complain about her adorably nicknamed boyfriend, "Pencil Dick" Dinklespiel.

> **You think:** Oh, my god, I am so tired. I guess this is part of my job, to pretend that this is fun. Surely she has a friend she can call?

> **Probable reality:** Your boss is a narcissistic wacko who has no friends, so she makes friends of her paid assistants. Unless you're a doctor or manage a disco, calls at midnight are

not generally part of the job. If it is to be part of your job, get it in writing, along with how much overtime it will cost your boss.

Your boss, "Fatso" Fields, chases you around his desk.

You think: What the fuh? This only happens in *New Yorker* cartoons from 1928! Will I get fired if I don't let him catch me? I must be wearing clothing that I didn't realize was suggestive.

Probable reality: Your boss has seen too many *New Yorker* cartoons from 1928, and chases all of his secretaries around his desk. Drop the dictation pad, hightail it past the Victrola, and get a new job.

Your boss constantly depends on you for tech support, since "you're so good at all that computer stuff."

You think: Wow, I must be scoring serious Brownie points helping my boss out so much with her computer!

Probable reality: Your boss is saving hundreds of dollars in tech support fees, because she doesn't have to hire a tech support guy. It's very nice of you to help out, but let your boss know if it's getting in the way of your work. If you really would rather not be doing tech support, pretend that a particular problem is beyond your expertise, and offer to call tech support for her.

Your boss tells you who she is feuding with that week, whether she thought her underarms were smelly that day, and whether

her sex life happens to be on an upswing. Your boss does not think this is too much information.

You think: It seems as if she is giving me too much information. But I guess she really likes to confide in me.

Probable reality: She is giving you too much information because she is a workaholic who has no social life. She knows she is crazy, but she is hoping that by sharing all this information with you, that you will feel too guilty to leave for a better job with an actual sane person.

There are many wonderful bosses out there in the workplace, so don't be discouraged if you should get stuck with a wacko your first time out of the gate. If running your boss's personal errands, taking calls at midnight, and "helping" to write her child's term paper was not in the original job description, you are within your rights to put your foot down. But sometimes a good boss is worth going that extra mile for. You may be gaining a wealth of knowledge and experience from your boss, and you may admire and/or genuinely like him or her. You may want to put in a little extra work because you see your boss putting in a little extra work, and because you are doing it for yourself as much as for your boss.

YOU AND YOUR MENTOR

Older bosses frequently mentor younger people, and valuable relationships are often forged. When the boss is generous and secure, it can work very well. It can also work well even if you are the only one who is generous and secure. But the relationship can also develop into a situation where boundaries become, well, somewhat blurred.

If you are a younger person working for an older boss/mentor, be clear about your career path and keep a balance between the relationship you have with your mentor and the single-minded pursuit of your career goals. Learn everything you can about the industry you are attempting to break into, and learn everything you can from your mentor, who should be helping you along your path.

The situation is designed to be less than permanent. Your boss knows that you will either be taking what you have learned with you when you take off to blaze your own trail somewhere else, or you will be taking his place. So stay as long as you are learning and growing, but know when the relationship has started affecting your mental health. Know when you've learned all you can. And when you do leave, try not to burn any bridges. Have a good exit strategy, and take your leave gracefully.

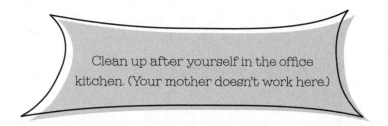

Clean up after yourself in the office kitchen. (Your mother doesn't work here.)

WE JUST DON'T WANT TO WAIT FOR YOU ANYMORE

Perhaps you have really, truly been working on that little lateness problem of yours, and you try your darnedest to show up pretty much on time to work and work-related meetings. Which is a good thing, because sooner or later someone might have realized that you are neither the CEO of your workplace nor a close relative of the boss, and thrown you out on your ear. Unless you are in fact the CEO, in which case you may arrive at noon, wearing your bathrobe and a fishing hat.

But do you still leave your friends hanging out to dry for long stretches because you can't manage to meet them when you promised you'd meet them? Dates with friends may not be important for your career, but friends are kind of a "must have" if you want to have a social life. And if you keep too many of them waiting for too long, they might become irritable, and not want to make plans with you anymore. That's right, even if you're very good looking.

Here's the thing; try to be more realistic about time. If you've arranged to meet with a friend, and it takes twenty minutes to get there, don't say, "I'll be over in twenty minutes" unless you have grabbed your coat and are literally walking out the door. Do not say "I'll be there in twenty minutes" if you are still in your pajamas and have to brush your teeth and take a shower and answer a few e-mails. Don't even say you'll be there in a half hour, unless you know you can be out the door in ten minutes flat. And for God's sake, stop showing up an hour late to dinner parties. It's rude is what it is, and it's not fair.

When you make people wait for you, you are implying that you are more important than they are, that your time is more precious, and that whatever they might have planned for the day doesn't matter. If I could reclaim the many hours I spent in my life waiting for friends who said they'd be there "in twenty minutes," I'd look quite a bit younger, and have enough time left for a manicure.

I know you don't mean to give that impression. I know you are a nice person, and that you try to be on time. I have a friend who used to be one of those infuriatingly time-challenged individuals. (Hi, Gail!) When I finally realized that sad fact about her, after spending far too much time twirling my thumbs and reheating dinners, I employed the following tactic: when she would call with the inevitable "I'll see you in twenty minutes," I would ask her if that was "Gail Time" or "Real Time." Eventually she resented my sarcastic tone and made an earnest attempt to have a less romantic relationship with the clock.

I hate having to lower my expectations of friends, but that's exactly what you must do if you have friends who continue to march to the beat of their own inner timepiece. Stop waiting and carry on with your life. Get things done that need doing. Catch up on your reading. (You must always bring a book or magazine when going to meet someone who is congenitally late.) If you made a meal for your tardy friend, and your friend is over an hour late, I think it's fair to go ahead and eat. If your friend was supposed to drop by an hour ago, and you have to leave to do some errands, go do your errands. Don't get mad, get busy.

And do what I do when I invite one of my incorrigibly late friends to dinner parties; if the party is called for seven o'clock, I tell him to come at six thirty. He'll usually show up a little after seven, none the wiser.

So whether it's setting your clock fifteen minutes ahead, or laying all your clothes out the night before, do what you have to do to be on time. If you are continually fifteen minutes late for appointments, you will just have to start giving yourself fifteen extra minutes lead time whenever you go to an appointment. It's so much better to have to wait for other people than to make others wait for you.

And if you are known to be a punctual person, you will be cut serious slack when you *are* eventually, for reasons out of your control, late. It can happen to the best of us—traffic jams, flat tires, nuclear disaster. You never know what you might encounter on your way to an appointment, so give yourself extra time and arrive relaxed and in control, hopefully having wiped that smug look off your face when the person you're meeting shows up five minutes late.

Driving: It's a STOP sign,
not a PAUSE sign.

Getting Acquainted with Your Kitchen

HOW TO BOIL AN EGG

I know. It seems simple. But you'd be surprised how many people don't know how to boil water, much less an egg. And you just don't want to find yourself, some bright morning when you're forty-two, reduced to staring at a stack of cookbooks, mystified and helpless, because your spouse went away for the weekend, along with the only brain in the house that knows how to make an egg salad sandwich. It happens, trust me.

Once you know how to boil an egg, you will have an easily made, inexpensive source of protein, not to mention the aforementioned egg salad sandwich, deviled eggs, and an essential ingredient in potato salad. A plain boiled egg with a sprinkle of salt makes a satisfying and nutritious meal, and you can keep them in the fridge for a few days, for those times when you are in a hurry but need something decent to eat.

So here's how you do it. Place your eggs in a pot and cover an inch or two with cold water. Turn on the heat and bring to a boil. As soon as the pot full of eggs comes to a boil, cover and turn off the heat. Let the eggs sit in the covered pot for seventeen minutes. Julia Child says seventeen minutes, so that's what we do. We do not argue with Julia. I'm sure if you took the eggs out at sixteen minutes, they'd be fine, but I do not want to risk Julia's wrath, even if she is no longer living. So, after seventeen minutes, take the pot over to the sink, drain the water out, and run cold water over the eggs to stop the cooking. When the eggs are cool enough to handle, peel the shells off, and rinse. You're done! That's it. Really, no big mystery.

If you don't intend to eat the eggs at one sitting, place the peeled eggs in a container, cover with cold water, and keep them, uncovered, in the refrigerator for up to three days.

TURN HARD-BOILED EGGS INTO AN EGG SALAD SANDWICH

Cut up or mash your hard-boiled eggs with a fork, mixing in enough mayonnaise, salt, and pepper to taste. You can add a few pinches of dried tarragon or dill. Spoon onto some bread, adding garnishes as desired.

TRANSFORM HARD-BOILED EGGS INTO DEVILED EGGS

1 dozen eggs

3 tablespoons butter, softened

About 1/3 cup mayonnaise

Salt & pepper, to taste

Paprika

After properly cooking your eggs, let them cool a bit, then peel and slice them in half. Remove the yolks and place in a bowl. Add the butter, mayonnaise, salt and pepper, and mash. If you are making very plain deviled eggs, you will spoon the fluffy yolk mixture back into the whites, and sprinkle paprika over the top, just like somebody's mom used to make. Or you may add tarragon or dill, chopped dill pickle, or chopped green olives. Experiment with chopped anchovy, capers, or pickled garlic. People love deviled eggs, and will consequently love the person who makes the deviled eggs. People will want to invite you over with your deviled eggs, because knowing how to make "great deviled eggs" imparts some sort of magic gloss over your person, making you appear not only skillful, but attractive. Also, I'd make more than a dozen if I were you. You cannot believe how people can pack these away.

MAYONNAISE! WHO KNEW IT HAD SO MANY USES?

Of course you knew that you could put mayonnaise on a turkey sandwich, in deviled eggs, and on a hamburger. (But this is true only if you grew up on the West Coast. "Ick," if you are an East Coaster.)

You were aware of its many gustatory uses, but did you know that you can get rid of split ends *and* the rings on your furniture with a simple application of this versatile goo? Do not hold the mayo!

You can use a regular jar of the supermarket's brand or you can go organic. It's also pretty easy to make your own mayonnaise. You'll know exactly what goes into it, and you might not smell as much like potato salad after the following hair application:

For Ratty, Dry, Saltwater-and-Sun-Damaged Hair: Starting with the ends, slather on the mayo, working up to the crown. Massage your scalp, for no reason other than it feels good. Now pile your hair up (if it's long) and either wrap it in plastic wrap or stick it under a shower cap. Let the mayo soak in while you go about your business. If you want "the works," mash half an avocado with a little plain yogurt and put it on your face for a nourishing mask. This is best done on a Saturday or Sunday when you won't be expecting any company. Now go rest your eyes for twenty minutes, then wipe that green stuff off your face, splashing with warm water. Eat the other half of the avocado with a dollop of that mayonnaise. Yum!

For Ratty, Dry, Wet-Beverage-Damaged Tables: Have too many clueless friends left their marks on your fab mid-century coffee table by setting down their cocktail glasses or moist beer bottles without a coaster underneath? Does your nice wood furniture have more rings than Liberace? Or maybe you found your furniture on the sidewalk on garbage day. That particular type of ring may be beyond this simple fix, but you can always try. Simply rub a glob of mayonnaise onto the ring and let it sit there for an hour or two. After it's been soaking for a while, get an old rag and spread the by-now melted mayo over the whole table. After another little while, take a dry, clean, soft cloth, and really rub that table until it's all buffed out. Pretty? Shiny? If the rings are still there, well, you may need to eventually have the whole thing refinished, or at least subject your piece of furniture to a gentle sand-ing, after which you can stain and finish with an appropriate stain and finish. But it's worth a try, because it has worked for me, and at the very least you'll end up with a gleaming, polished piece of furniture. Albeit one that smells a little like a deli.

FABULOUS HOMEMADE MAYONNAISE SAUCES

HOMEMADE MAYONNAISE

This can easily be made with a wire whisk, which I really prefer, as there are fewer things to wash up afterward.

    2 large eggs
    2 teaspoons Dijon mustard
    1 teaspoon salt
    1/2 teaspoon freshly ground white pepper
    3 teaspoons white wine vinegar
    2 cups peanut, corn, or olive oil
    2 to 3 tablespoons freshly squeezed lemon juice

Place everything but the oil and lemon juice into a bowl and whisk together. Add the oil, first in a drizzle, then in a thin, steady stream, while whisking furiously with your other hand. When all the oil has been added, continue whisking until it starts to really thicken. Add lemon juice to your taste. If the sauce is too thick, thin with hot water or lemon juice. If too thin, whisk a little longer.

Yield: 2 1/2 cups

While your hair is marinating and your table is soaking, you can use what's left of your mayonnaise to make the following delicious sauces!

Aioli: Aioli is just a garlicky mayonnaise. It's especially delicious as a dip for French fries, but also a tasty addition to fish, sandwiches, poached or boiled eggs, or vegetables.

4 cloves garlic
1/8 teaspoon salt
1/2 teaspoon lemon juice
1 to 2 tablespoons olive oil

In a small bowl, mash the garlic cloves, salt, and lemon juice together. Add the olive oil, enough to make a soft consistency. Whisk into your homemade mayonnaise.

A Dipping Sauce for Artichokes: Squeeze the juice of half a lemon (or more, to taste) into a cup or two of mayonnaise, depending on how many people you're feeding. Whisk together and grind in pepper and a pinch of salt to taste. A dash of curry powder is optional.

A Sauce for Poached Salmon: Add one diced red bell pepper and a handful of chopped fresh dill to a cup or so of mayonnaise. Serve over poached salmon.

Dressing for Poached Chicken: Add a diced mango and several dashes of hot sauce to a cup or two of mayonnaise. For a shortcut, just mix some mango salsa in with the mayonnaise. This is great on chicken and fish.

SAUCE FOR ASPARAGUS

You can pour a nice homemade hollandaise sauce over asparagus, but if you don't have the time or inclination to make a homemade hollandaise sauce, simply put a cup of mayonnaise into a bowl and whisk in:

2 tablespoons warmed and softened unsalted butter

1 tablespoon or so of dried tarragon

1 or 2 dashes of cayenne pepper

A squeeze of lemon

HOW IN THE WORLD DO I POACH A CHICKEN? WHAT IS A POACHED SALMON?

You need to cook, because you're a grown-up. You really cannot ignore the inevitable. You can pretend to be a hip, skateboarding, MP3-playing teenager until you're forty-eight. Many people do. But if you wait until you're old and gray to learn how to cook, you will be missing out on many years of impressing dates, sharing good food with friends, having dinner parties, and of course nourishing yourself. Not to mention the money you'll save! You can make sumptuous meals for yourself at home, salting away the thousands of dollars you would spend on eating out for every meal.

So, we'll start with something simple. If you can poach a chicken breast and you can poach a piece of salmon, you will be able to make a million different meals. You can poach a whole pile of chicken breasts and make a different dish every night for a week. With a pile of chicken breasts you can eat sliced chicken breast served cold or hot, with any of the aforementioned sauces, or you can turn those chicken breasts into:

* Cold chicken curry salad!
* Chinese chicken salad!
* Chicken sandwiches!

* Throw some diced poached chicken on top of any salad, when you need some protein!
* Throw some diced poached chicken into soup!

Or do what a million tired mothers have done throughout the ages, and make a good old-fashioned chicken a la king. Which is basically chicken with mushroom soup sauce. Sauté a handful of chopped onions and some mushrooms in a pan with a little olive oil until they're browned. Add some of your leftover chopped poached chicken and a can of mushroom soup. Add a dash of sherry if you want to get fancy. If you keep no sherry around, a dash of wine or vermouth will do. Serve over toast or English muffins.

Poached Salmon: With several pieces of poached salmon, you can eat cold poached salmon with any one of the lovely mayonnaise sauces listed previously, or:

* Add cold poached salmon to any salad!
* Put some chunks of poached salmon on a simple pasta with olive oil and garlic and capers!
* Add some poached salmon to your cold gazpacho!
* Make a poached salmon sandwich with watercress!
* Get a bag of arugula, rinse a handful, and toss it up with the juice of half a lemon, a few dashes of olive oil, maybe some chopped red onion and avocado. Top with your cold poached salmon and you have got a meal!

So, to poach a piece of salmon, do this:

1. Fill a pot with cold water. Add a bay leaf, some peppercorns, and a cup of white wine. Throw in some chopped onion or

parsley, if it's on hand. If you want to use half water and half chicken broth or vegetable broth, you can do that, too; it will all help impart more flavor.

2. Turn the heat on high and bring the water or broth to a boil. Place the salmon pieces gently into the boiling water with a spatula, making sure they are covered by liquid. Cover the pot and turn off the heat.

3. Let sit for exactly 30 minutes, then remove the salmon and place it on a plate to cool off. That is all there is to it. It is incredibly easy, and the salmon ends up being cooked perfectly. If you want to eat it warm, eat it warm. If you want cold poached salmon, let it cool off a bit before you put it in the refrigerator.

Poached Chicken: For poached chicken, you do much the same thing:

1. Fill the pot with water or broth, a bit of onion, a bay leaf, and peppercorns. Experiment with adding rosemary or tarragon.

2. Crank up the heat, bringing the liquid to a boil, and place the chicken breasts into the pot, making sure the liquid covers the chicken. Simmer for 5 minutes, turn the breasts over, and cover the pot.

3. Turn off the heat and let the covered pot sit for exactly 30 minutes. Your chicken should be absolutely moist and delicious. How easy was that?

MEA CULPA, VEGGIES!

If you are a vegetarian, I'm sure I have totally grossed you out and am truly, truly sorry. If you are a vegetarian, I will assume that you already know how to eat, unless you are one of those cheese vegetarians, who thinks that being a vegetarian means getting to live on cheesy snacks and never having to actually eat a vegetable.

Whether you are a vegetarian or not, you still have to eat vegetables. You can't just suck back an overdressed salad once in a while and call it a day. If you cannot bear broccoli, if you cringe at cauliflower, if eggplant makes you anxious, try this:

Roast your vegetables! It is really kind of a fall and winter thing, but I roast vegetables in the summer, too. You can serve a big platter of them to a party at room temperature with feta cheese sprinkled on top, or roast just enough for yourself, with a little left over to eat the next day. For some reason, vegetables that many people dislike turn into sweet, edible bites of sheer vegetable heaven when roasted. You really should try it. And if you invite a friend over for dinner, your friend will be amazed and want you to explain how to roast vegetables, and you can pass on your wisdom. And your friend will pass on the knowledge, and that friend will tell another friend. Pretty soon everyone will be roasting squash and asparagus and tomatoes, and actually eating vegetables, and the world will be a happier, healthier place.

So, heat the oven to 450°F. Sometimes I roast things at 500°, sometimes I go to 400°F. You will have fun experimenting. But to start off, know that little, watery things, like cherry tomatoes, will roast in about 15 minutes, broccoli will take a little longer, and the smaller you chop everything the faster it will cook. If I have larger chunks of starchier vegetables, acorn squash or banana squash or yams, I put them in a separate pan and roast them longer than my pan of broccoli, onions, and peppers. Chunks of potatoes take longer than broccoli but not as long as squash. Make sure all your vegetables are coated with a little olive oil and a sprinkling of salt. Use these basic guidelines, or one of the recipes that follows. And I really mean this, yum.

OVEN-ROASTED POTATOES, TURNIPS, AND RUTABAGA

1 1/2 pounds baby potatoes, such as Baby Dutch, or small new potatoes, halved, or regular potatoes cut up into 1-inch pieces, peeled or
   unpeeled
2 small turnips, peeled and cut in 3/4-inch cubes
2 medium rutabagas, peeled and cut in 3/4-inch cubes
1 onion, peeled and cut into large chunks
3 or more whole cloves garlic in their skins
1 teaspoon salt, or to taste
1 teaspoon freshly ground black pepper, or to taste
Olive oil, to coat

Preheat the oven to 475°F. In a 2- to 3-quart baking dish, toss the vegetables, salt and pepper, and the olive oil. Roast for about 45 minutes, stirring a few times, until vegetables are tender and lightly browned. Stick a knife into a few of the vegetable chunks to check for doneness. Slip the roasted garlic cloves out of their skins, coarsely chop, and toss back in. Serves 6 to 8.

ROASTED CHERRY TOMATOES

This is a really easy side dish to make when you don't know what in the hell to serve with your main course. Preheat the oven to 500°F. Rinse and dry a basket or two of cherry tomatoes, then toss with a little olive oil and salt. Place in a large, shallow roasting pan so that you've got one layer. A cookie sheet will work, if it has sides, or a jelly roll pan. Roast for 15 minutes. You can sprinkle with a little feta cheese, or just serve as is, hot, warm, or at room temperature. Sweet!

VEGETABLES THAT GENERALLY TASTE MUCH BETTER ROASTED IN THE OVEN, IF YOU ASK ME

Broccoli
Cauliflower
Asparagus
Eggplant
Zucchini
Turnips
Rutabaga
Onions (get sweeter)
Garlic (becomes mellower)
Squash (gets all sugary and delicious)

YOUR OWN FAST FOOD KITCHEN: A WORD ON TRANSFORMING RAW MATERIALS INTO A LOVELY FEAST

Instead of constantly purchasing packaged, prepared food, or always buying bottled salad dressing, why not stock your pantry with some basic raw materials, and try cooking from scratch once in a while? When you're really pressed for time, sure, throw that frozen meal into the microwave. But there is no need to make a habit of it, and you'll discover a whole new world of tastes if you can learn to transform some simple foods into a meal. It's easy to make your own salad dressing, so much tastier, and if you keep a few basic things on hand, it's not at all difficult to throw together.

A SIMPLE VINAIGRETTE

This is a bare-bones recipe for a basic, all-purpose vinaigrette, which you can vary as you wish. Its beauty lies solely in the quality of your ingredients, so it's worth keeping some good extra virgin olive oil around the house, along with a few nice vinegars. The usual suggestion in vinaigrette recipes is 1 part vinegar to 3 parts oil, but that can make a very vinegary vinaigrette. You can always add more vinegar or lemon but you can't take it out, so start with much less, and add to taste.

1/2 tablespoon finely minced shallot, green onion, or garlic
1/2 tablespoon Dijon-type mustard
1/4 teaspoon salt

1/2 tablespoon freshly squeezed lemon juice

1/2 tablespoon wine vinegar: red, white, or sherry

1/3 to 1/2 cup excellent extra virgin olive oil

Freshly ground black pepper

Either shake all the ingredients together in a screw-top jar, or mix them in a bowl as follows. Stir the shallots, scallions, or garlic together with the mustard and salt. Whisk in the lemon juice and vinegar, and when well blended, start whisking in the oil by droplets to form a smooth emulsion. Beat in the freshly ground pepper. Taste (dip a lettuce leaf into the dressing) and correct the seasoning with salt, pepper, and/or drops of lemon juice.

Experiment! Use balsamic vinegar, aged sherry vinegar, or fruit-flavored vinegar. Use all lemon juice instead of vinegar, which is delicious. Add more or less garlic instead of the shallot, finely minced onion, finely chopped tomatoes, dried basil, or assorted herbs to add variety to your dressing. Chop up a grapefruit and throw it into your salad, juice and all, with a little olive oil drizzled on top. Delicious!

My friend Geri says: "Heat up leftover pizza in a nonstick skillet on top of the stove, set heat to medium-low, and heat till warm. This keeps the crust crispy. No soggy microwaved pizza. I saw this on the cooking channel and it really works." I guess someone has the time to sit around and watch the cooking channel.

Make French Toast! Why? Because it's delicious, and so easy to make. And you need to eat breakfast, you really do. I know you just like to grab a muffin and a latte sometime around eleven o'clock, but you need a little protein to start off the day.

So, to make French toast for just yourself, crack one or two eggs into a bowl, mix with about a quarter cup of milk, add a dash of cinnamon, a splash of vanilla extract (and almond extract, if you have it), and some grated nutmeg. Whisk it all together and put pieces of bread in to soak. I like to cut a large piece of bread into halves or quarters, that's just the way I am.

The longer the bread soaks, the gooier it is in the middle, which is a good thing. We like the gooey center. Turn the heat up high to get the pan nice and hot, add a little butter or olive oil to the pan, and then pop in the batter-soaked bread. Turn the heat down to medium. Your French toast should be nice and browned on the edges, and still a bit runny inside, so don't cook it for too long. If you're making French toast for friends, just add another egg or two per person, more milk and flavorings, and of course, more bread.

If you make too much batter, you can save it in the fridge for up to three days, making it that much easier for you to make French toast on those days when you just don't feel like putting in the effort. And what makes it even easier is, you can use *stale* bread! In fact, stale bread is preferred. Oh, those French. Just be sure to cut the green mold off if it's been sitting for too long.

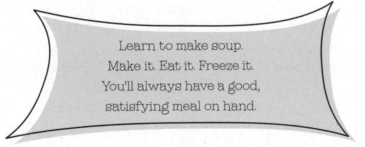

Learn to make soup.
Make it. Eat it. Freeze it.
You'll always have a good,
satisfying meal on hand.

A REALLY EASY SOUP
(IN CASE YOU'RE PRESSED FOR TIME AND CAN'T SPEND HOURS MAKING A CHICKEN STOCK.)

You can turn this into a kind of a "kitchen sink" soup, throwing in whatever vegetables you have on hand and pureeing them once they've cooked and softened. But the basic broth is made by sautéing one or more onions until translucent and golden, throwing in a handful of garlic cloves, and pouring a carton or two of (preferably organic) chicken or vegetable broth into the pot. Add your chopped vegetables, cook until they're softened, and puree. A bag of frozen baby peas will make a nice green spring pea soup. Use a bag or two of frozen corn, and you've got corn chowder, with the addition of a splash of cream and some minced red pepper, for color. Puree cooked zucchini, then add a can of kidney beans, chopped tomatoes, and some cooked pasta for a faux minestrone. Cook and puree a whole, chopped cauliflower in your onion stock, and top with a good, grated parmesan cheese. Broccoli, a vegetable many people resist, becomes mild and tasty when pureed into a flavorful stock. Add a few potatoes and top with grated cheddar cheese! Yum. The possibilities are endlessly delicious. You can't go too wrong if you make a nice base with lots of garlic and onion. Season to taste with salt and pepper, and experiment with a variety of herbs to give your soups a distinct flavor. Tarragon in a potato soup is a nice touch, as is oregano and basil with minestrone and Italian squashes.

Tip for the Lazy Cook: A stick blender is an indispensable tool, especially for those of us who hate the washing-up part of cooking. Rather than having to pour hot soup into a blender—a messy and possibly dangerous proposition—simply plug in your stick blender, submerge it into your soup, and turn it on. Use a gentle mashing motion to blend up all the bits (careful not to lift it from the soup while it's turned on or you'll find yourself with a wall of savory spin-art), and you've got an easy puree, with only one pot to clean.

Kitchen Tip: Keep aluminum foil on hand for when you really want to make those double chocolate tollhouse cookies, but don't have a cookie sheet. Simply cover your oven racks with foil, place the cookie dough directly on the foil (you might need to put a little grease on it, depending how much butter is in the batter), presto, hot cookies with very little cleanup. And you can reuse or recycle your aluminum foil!

My friend Geri says: "To warm bread, biscuits, pancakes, or muffins that were refrigerated, place them in a microwave with a cup of water. The increased moisture will keep the food moist and help it reheat faster." I don't have a microwave; thank goodness someone knows about these things.

MORE KITCHEN TIPS

* Always use unsalted butter; that way you can control the saltiness yourself.
* Keep extra virgin olive oil on hand for dressing salads, dipping bread, sauces, sautéing, and a million other things not limited to makeup removal and hot-oil hair treatment.
* Grape seed oil is great for cooking, because it can take higher temperatures. And it's good for you.
* A small wire whisk is indispensable.
* Capers! Just because.
* Horseradish! Ditto.
* There are some great hot sauces out there, and they are a wonderful addition to any kitchen. One of my favorites is called Mango Meltdown—it's unbelievably delicious on steak, fish, and eggs, and can be added to mayonnaise for a lovely sweet/

spicy mayonnaise sauce. Another favorite is called Dave's Total Insanity. It should be used sparingly, but if you like things spicy, it's a must-have in the kitchen. A drop on your eggs goes a long way, and you'll need only a few dashes for a vat of chili. Keep a fresh jar of cayenne pepper, which is indispensable for adding spice to any dish.

* Google! For any recipe under the sun. Want to attempt to recreate that delicious tamale pie that used to be served at summer camp? Well, I Googled it and had tamale pie recipes coming out of my ears! If you really liked a certain rum drink, or flourless chocolate cake from some obscure restaurant, I guarantee you'll be able to find it, or a reasonable facsimile, on Google.

* Despite what somebody told you once, don't keep your coffee beans in the freezer. Keep them in a cool, dark cupboard to keep them as fresh as possible, and grind them as you use them.

* Always keep a few kinds of interesting mustards around.

* Always wash bagged lettuce. It freshens it up and theoretically washes off bacteria it might have accumulated from sitting in a plastic bag. Buy organic if possible, and support local farmers!

* Also, when I buy hearts of romaine, I like to cut the end off the stalk and soak the heads in a bowl of water, as if you're soaking flowers. Lettuce is mostly water, and the soaking really plumps up the leaves.

* Fresh nutmeg is so much better than ground nutmeg. Just buy whole nutmeg, grate as much as you need, and put what's left of the nut back into its jar. Grate it into your French toast batter, into turkey stuffing, into chicken broth, and of course into pumpkin and apple pies.

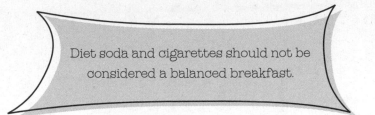

Diet soda and cigarettes should not be considered a balanced breakfast.

A DAMN FINE CUP OF JOE

Do you make your coffee in the microwave? Not to be a pill, but I have nothing good to say about coffee made in a microwave oven. In fact I am just about speechless on the subject of microwaved coffee. And don't even mention coffee that was made five hours ago, and then reheated in a microwave. You have, sadly, possibly never tasted a proper cup of coffee. But once you have had a proper cup of coffee, you will be amazed that you ever put a nice cup of coffee in a microwave oven, and you will be loath to do it ever again.

First, you want to purchase very fresh whole beans, which means you will need a decent coffee grinder. There are two kinds of grinders, a blade grinder and a burr grinder, the less expensive being a blade grinder. With a blade grinder, you control the fineness of the grind, depending on what type of coffeemaker you're using, but blade grinders do have a tendency to heat up the beans or grind them to powder, which sometimes makes for an inconsistent brew. A burr grinder crunches the beans up nicely and gives you a consistent grind. A conical burr grinder is the best, being less noisy and less messy, but they are also the priciest. You can research grinders on the Internet, or go to your local cookware store and ask some questions.

Next, you should figure out what type of coffeemaker you want to use. I am a big fan of the French press, which is now much more avail-

A fine cup of Joe

able than it used to be, and can be found in a few different sizes. You can even get thermal ones, in case you want to keep your coffee warm for a few hours. Another fine choice would be a drip coffee pot, like a Chemex, very mid-century chic, which uses a filter (paper, cloth, or metal mesh) to make coffee.

So let's say you've wisely opted for the French press, since that's the one I know most about, and incidentally, makes a damn fine cup of java.

If you buy coffee that's already been ground, it will go stale in about ten minutes. I know you'll think it abnormally picky, but stale coffee really does affect the taste, so always buy whole beans, and grind the beans up while your water is on the stove. Heat your (preferably filtered) water in a kettle on the stove until just before it boils. If you let it boil, just let it sit for a few minutes to come off the boil. Pour it over the grounds that have been put in the bottom of your French press (the general rule of thumb is 2 tablespoons of ground coffee for every 6 ounces of water) and stir. I use a chopstick, you can use a long wooden spoon, just make sure you didn't ladle onions with it the night before. Avoid stirring it with metal, at least that's what I've heard. (And to be really picky, grind your beans for no more than twelve seconds—if you have a blade grinder—for a French press or drip. Look, you might as well do it right if you're going to all this trouble with the fresh ground beans and the coffee press and all.) After stirring, let the coffee steep (sit still) for 4 to 5 minutes before plunging the filter.

Please, I beg of you, don't make a nice pot of coffee and then heat it up again two hours later. Likewise, if you use an automatic drip coffeemaker, don't leave your coffee cooking for too long on the burner. "Too long" means that after fifteen to twenty minutes, that lovely dark reddish brown color disappears, and you have a pot of old-timey heartburn. If you have a lot of coffee left over, save it in a carafe and put it in the fridge for iced coffee. If you want to keep your pot of coffee hot, pour it into a thermos.

If you are a hard-core coffee drinker, or wish to be a hard-core coffee drinker, there are also coffee roasters available for home use. You can even roast green coffee beans in a hot-air popcorn maker, but I'm not going to go into how in the world you might go about that, at least not until I've had several more cups of coffee.

DO DISHES *WITHOUT* A DISHWASHER?

So there you are, in your new apartment. You've just had friends over, you actually tackled a modest dinner, and then you all made home-made cookies. You really want to clean up the five cookie sheets, three dough-and-chocolate encrusted mixing bowls, mixing spoons, electric blender, and three chocolate-encrusted plates, plus the five plates left-over from dinner, smeared with coagulated tomato sauce that has by this time indelibly hardened into a mass. But you can't open the dish-washer. Or it's broken. Or you can't figure out how the twisty knobby thing turns. Do you leave this pile of dirty plates just sitting there? Do you throw your hands up in despair, foiled once again by modern tech-nology? Do you wait until your mother comes over and does your dishes for you? No! No, you don't.

Now listen, before dishwashers were invented and popularized for home use, many people had sinks. I will continue on the assumption that you are at least the proud owner or renter of a sink. A very efficient way to do the dishes—some say the best way to do dishes—is right at your fingertips, by simply making use of your sink and the water that comes right out of your tap. That's right! You can actually wash your dishes by hand. And I am going to tell you how to do it without wasting nine hundred gallons of water. A double sink makes this even easier, but let's just say you have a single kitchen sink. Even a bathroom sink will do.

First, you will need a container of dishwashing liquid, a sponge, and some kind of rubber plug for your sink. Squirt a few squirts of the dishwashing liquid into your plugged sink and turn on the hot water. As the sink is filling, scrape all the food that has been encrusted or is clinging to the plates and bowls into the garbage. (If you have a garbage disposal, you may utilize this amenity before you fill the sink. Use with cold water, please!) If you have a double sink, make sure the other half is really clean, and fill it with plain hot water. If you don't have a double sink, fill a really big pot or bowl with hot water, and place it next to the sink.

First, submerge the least disgusting items, like cups and glasses, into the hot, soapy water and gently scrub clean. Then rinse by dipping them into the plain, unsoapy water until they squeak when you run your fingers around the rims. Place the squeaky-clean dishes upside down on a fresh dish towel that has been set on some counter or other.

If all the plates are encrusted with, say, spaghetti sauce, stack them and place the whole stack into the hot, soapy water. While the plates soak, put all the silverware into a large mug, or other container. Submerge the container into the soapy water, and then scrub each fork and spoon and knife with your sponge, dropping each into the plain rinse water as it's finished. Rinse the silverware container and fill with hot water. Fish out the silverware from the rinse water, and place into the smaller container full of hot water, for an extra rinse.

While you have been blithely cleaning your utensils, all the disgusting stuff crusted on to your plates will have miraculously soaked off, rendering them a cinch to clean. So, one plate at a time, gently scrub the residual gunk off the plates, then rinse, by dipping into the unsoapy water, and stack. Dry with a clean dish towel, and replace on your shelf. Voilà!

If your party has gone on until all hours and you simply cannot face cleaning the dishes, at least fill up the sink with hot soapy water and stick your dishes in it. You will thank me in the morning. Yes, in the morning you are going to have to stick your hand into a sink full of cold, greasy water to unplug the plug, but the discomfort will last only a moment, and it will be well worth it in the long run. After draining the sink and refilling it with warm, soapy water, scrubbing the dishes will be a mere formality after their overnight soak.

Many people who have dishwashers feel the need to wash the dishes thoroughly before loading them. This is a tremendous waste of water, and totally unnecessary, but still, everyone does it. They run scalding water at full bore over every dish, and then load the dishes into the dishwasher. If you own a dishwasher, or are helping friends wash their dishes and feel you must subject the dishes to a thorough scrub before the machine wash, then why not save a bazillion gallons of water by using the hand-washing technique described above? Fill up the sink with hot water (although the soap won't be necessary) and gently submerge the whole pile of dishes, cups, and silverware into the water. You'll have time to visit with your friends a little more before coaxing the gunk off the dishes and loading the washer, and you will have used only a few gallons of water instead of hundreds, which will make you feel not only efficient, but quite virtuous.

Get Dressed!

Of course, the world would be a fabulous place if women wore little black dresses and red lipstick on a more regular basis. It would be a lovely thing if men and women put a little thought into wearing clothing appropriate for whatever the occasion. What I am trying to say here is, if you're invited to an evening party, sweatpants and a t-shirt might give your host the impression that you weren't looking forward to the event as much as you might have been. It looks as if you really didn't care in the least bit. If you really don't care in the least bit, then don't go to the party. If you do care and you really do want to go to the party, then show your enthusiasm by getting dressed.

JUST SAY NO TO CULOTTES: REJECTING THE TYRANNY OF FASHION

There you are, at the shopping mall, or that cute boutique, and the resident mannequins are all outfitted beautifully in perfect ensembles. The trousers hang perfectly, the t-shirts and jackets drape in an insouciant manner that make you immediately want to purchase the complete ensemble directly off the mannequin. Resist this urge.

Mannequins, much like Barbie dolls, have figures that are rarely found in nature. The exact same outfit displayed on a manufactured plaster body—as attractive as that body may be—might not look quite the same on a live human, especially one with measurements on a more, er, human scale.

Mannequins look good in everything, much like your lanky, six foot two friend who can wear bright red skinny trousers and a sky-blue polyester golf shirt with a giant pointy collar. He wears it ironically. It looks amusing on his gorgeous frame. On a shorter perhaps more portly man, the ensemble would not have that same kicky, artsy flair. In fact, a shorter, stocky man might look rather as if he didn't quite know how to dress himself, as if he was recently released from that nice halfway house and bought the first thing he pulled off the rack at the Salvation Army.

Mannequins look good in everything, and they also have professional fashion people dressing them. If you buy the ensemble directly off the mannequin at the store, trust me, *it will not look the same on you*, and you will be sorry.

Models, much like mannequins, are really, really different from you and me. Well, maybe not you, but certainly from me. However, their appearance on the pages of magazines continue to fool me into thinking that I will look exactly the same as they do as soon as I put on the exact same outfit.

How do they do it? Models are clearly bred on special farms, or in sterilized tanks, somewhere in Czechoslovakia, Sweden, and the Midwest of the United States. They are especially raised to look fabulous while wearing burlap, stonewashed denim, and "retro" fashions from the 1980s, a feat that we mere mortals dare not try at home. Their shoulders are designed to match the line of a beautiful handmade wooden hanger, and their waists and legs are individually elongated, so as to show off the swing of that layered peasant skirt. Put a layered peasant skirt on any regular woman, and we will look, not surprisingly, like peasants, matronly refugees from Eastern bloc countries swimming in big, ruffled skirts. You can be in your twenties, and theoretically look good in a paper bag—and you will look matronly. Ruffles do not become the average body type, and even with the intrigue of the shoulder-baring peasant neckline, the added bulk around the thigh area surely defeats the purpose.

Look at yourself with a steely gaze not bathed in gauze, but drenched in reality. That blousy bubble dress may look all bohemian and carefree on a six foot tall model, but it may not have quite the same effect on a roundish five foot two frame. I have a friend who has a body born to wear high couture; she could wear denim gauchos and still look like Audrey Hepburn. If I were to wear the same ensemble, the average onlooker would avert his horrified gaze and frantically hunt for loose change to give me.

But I am putty in the hands of fashion marketing professionals, and after an hour or so of staring at pretty girls in pretty clothes, I am convinced that the clothes they are wearing will somehow look the same on me. Do not make the mistakes I have made. You will find yourself with a closet full of fabulous clothing you will only be able to stare at longingly, until your taller, thinner friends come over. You will make them try on your clothes, and your clothes will look so much better on them that you will willingly hand over your beautiful frocks, pencil skirts, and trousers, one by one.

Assess your fine qualities, and make the most of them, using your imagination and innate esthetic sense. If you have no imagination or innate esthetic sense, develop some immediately. You do not need a million dollars and a personal stylist to look like a million bucks. In fact, it *used* to be that actors, actresses, and other assorted celebrities did not have personal stylists, and hence, the Academy Awards presentation used to be much more fun to watch. The stars were more prone to showing up in evening wear of their own choosing and/or design; sequined pantsuits, poufy ball gowns emblazoned with giant embroidered piano keys, or anything worn by Cher. Some of the outfits were insanely ugly, and some worked beautifully, in an awful way, and a few were accidentally lovely, but at least people had their own personal style, and didn't pay someone to have it for them.

Then someone figured out how to make money off style-challenged celebrities, suddenly everyone got all tasteful, and the fun went right out of it. No more feathered headdresses and see-through harem pants. No more raccoon eyes and bad turquoise prom dresses. No more starlets living their giddy sartorial dreams.

Figure out a style that works for you and your own special body type. Do not become a slave to the merry fashion marketeers, who will insist that you need to spend gobs of money every "season" in order to be a fashionable person. Fashion can be whatever you decide it is, and you can be terribly chic without spending your rent money, or getting into debt up to your eyeballs. This is not an invitation to prance about in your stretched-out sweats and torn wife beater, but you needn't become so tasteful that you lose all sense of individuality.

And individual style is a lot less expensive than following the herd. You may think you need the three-thousand-dollar clutch purse with the giant Gucci insignia, or that Prada shoes are the only kind in which you can possibly ever feel comfortable. But honestly, do you know how much rent those people have to pay to get those fancy addresses? Do you realize you are paying heart-stopping prices for that merchandise so that large companies can continue to pay hugely inflated rents so that you, and a bunch of Japanese tourists, can continue to purchase their expensive brands? Do not become one of P. T. Barnum's all-day suckers. You can buy a lot of personal style for the price of one Manolo, with enough left over for a nice sushi dinner. Not to mention how much you can tuck away into that little retirement fund you'll now be able to start.

FROM THE DEPARTMENT OF DUH

Every few years, those nice people who are in the business of marketing fashion will attempt to convince you that you must buy "skinny pants." Many people will then madly rush out and buy "skinny black pants," or "skinny jeans" or stovepipe trousers and then get home and wonder what the hell they were thinking. As if it weren't abundantly obvious, you must actually *be skinny* to have skinny pants still look like skinny pants once they're on you. Skinny pants, sadly, do not actually make a person skinny. Many will buy, but only a handful of tall, gangly nineteen-year-olds will be able to pull off the skinny pants look. When the dust has cleared, the marketing people will move on to high-waisted-wide-leg trousers, low-rise gauchos, or whatever else amuses them. And don't think they aren't amused. "We changed the name to 'short shorts' and got a bunch of women to buy hot pants! Again! Suck-ahs!" I'm just saying.

SEEMINGLY ANACHRONISTIC SKILLS
WE SHOULD ALL HAVE: LAUNDRY AND IRONING!

Notice that I cleverly combined the laundry and ironing sections, thereby alleviating the pressure to come up with long, descriptive chapters on each subject. I mean, what can one say about doing laundry, other than you need to know how to do it if you want clean clothes?

Try to use biodegradable laundry detergent. Try to save up and do a large load, so you don't waste water doing nine loads of two t-shirts each. You can wash single items in your sink, if you really need something the next day. Separate your whites from your colors. Launder your colors in cold water to keep them from fading. If you live in a temperate climate, you will not only save tons of energy but you will extend the life of your clothing if you hang your wet laundry in the sun to dry. Fine fabrics, anything with elastic, and bras are much better off being air dried. So even if you live in a cold and rainy place, you can hang those delicate items on a hanger to dry indoors. (In the shower or above the bath, to catch drips.)

Or get yourself a magical laundry elf, which I did quite by accident. I had no idea when I got married that my husband would love doing the laundry so much. Thank goodness, because if it were only me, I might be more apt to just buy more clothes rather than tackle that moldering pile of whites hiding in the corner. So we divide up our chores in a way that suits us. I don't love doing laundry and dishes and he appears to enjoy doing both. I love to cook and don't mind cleaning bathrooms, so I take on those tasks, and everyone's happy and not coming down with cholera. You may be able to work out the same kind of arrangement with your roommate, if you have one.

So, to the ironing. Okay, I hate to iron. I haven't owned an iron since you were in diapers. It is tedious and annoying. But if I had to do it, I know how. Please don't make me. I also know that I can send stuff off to the cleaners and they'll do a wonderful job of it. Still, it's good to know a thing or two about ironing, one of many seemingly anachronistic skills that everyone ought to have. If nothing else, you will be a more interesting person for it, and will become known as someone with possibly the most outdated but quite the most interesting life skills. "Hey!" they'll say, when you arrive at the door. "Brandon's

Harness the Power of the Sun.

If you use a Clothesline instead of a DRYER for 6 MONTHS out of the year, you can ELIMINATE 700 pounds of carbon dioxide emissions.

Especially those JEANS which take FOREVER to dry.

here! Whoa, Brandon, did you *iron* that shirt yourself? Hey, ladies, Brandon irons *and* knows how to sew curtains and deep fry a turkey! Come on in!" I prefer linen shirts that are slightly rumpled, because you can iron a linen shirt for an hour, but an hour after you put it on it will wrinkle right up. That's the nature of linen. Still, if you like that sort of thing, a crisp, white linen shirt can be yours—that is if you own a white linen shirt—and of course, an iron. Ironing works on cotton shirts and khaki pants, although I wouldn't advise ironing your jeans, because if creased jeans were ever fashionable, they aren't now. Some people iron their sheets and pillowcases. Some iron their underthings. I will leave it to you to decide how much time you have in a day to devote to pursuing such thankless tasks, but then again, some find satisfaction in cleaning grout with a toothbrush, and I'm not about to tell them to stop. Iron your socks, if it makes you feel complete.

You'll be able to find an inexpensive, folding ironing board at any store that sells house wares, and you can assume that a steam iron will be lurking somewhere nearby. Look, ironing is one of those black holes in my education. I have a vague recollection of ironing something, sometime, a long, long time ago, but it really is not my cup of tea. Your best bet is to ask your mom or a friend how to iron that shirt. I can draw a few simple diagrams, but I just don't know how much good they'll do. Ironing is something you really have to experience. In a pinch, you can hang your wrinkled garment in the bathroom near the open shower door, and take a nice hot shower.

If you have a clothes dryer, you can throw the wrinkled article of clothing into your hot dryer for five to ten minutes; although it won't be pressed, the heat will take the wrinkles out. Just be sure to take the garment out and hang it up (or put it on) while it's still hot, so it won't get new wrinkles from cooling off while crumpled up in the dryer.

THINGS YOU CAN DO WHILE IRONING
* Blast music (Iron Butterfly?).
* Listen to the audio book of *War and Peace*.
* Download a big file or update computer programs.
* Watch an old movie (avoid thrillers).
* Soap operas were originally created to be a nondangerous diversion for the oft-ironing housebound housewife, but they are pretty much terrible. Rent the entire *Dark Shadows* gothic soap opera series, instead. It's beyond delicious.

WHY YOU NEED TO KNOW HOW TO SEW ON A BUTTON

Well, they do occasionally fall off. And you can walk around without buttons, which I have done, but why? You are only postponing the inevitable by pulling that shirt closed with a safety pin, when it is so easy, really, to sew the button back on. Okay, look, I don't like sewing on buttons any more than I like ironing. But I had to fire that charming young thing whose job it was to peel my grapes, do my grocery shopping, scrub my shower, and sew on my buttons. Okay, I had to kill her, she was really getting on my nerves with her cheerful humming and "You go girl!" attitude, and she was all, like, "Don't you love to work out?" every minute. Plus, I'm supposed to make her lunch? Hello? So now I have to sew on my own buttons. Damn it all!

This is a needle

THE EYE of the Needle

A BUTTON

This is thread

To THREAD A NEEDLE means to put the thread through the hole in the needle.

a single thread

KNOT THE END.

KNOT

a double thread

Bring needle up through one hole and down through the other,

up and around several times.

Knot it under the button by bringing the needle through the thread on the underside of the button.

Before

after

Portrait
of a Safety Pin

Tip: Pin a small safety pin to the seam of your hem and you will not have a clingy skirt or dress. Same thing works with slacks that cling when wearing panty hose, if anyone wears panty hose anymore. Place pin in seam of slacks and like magic, the static is gone. Eerie!

A NOTE TO (MOSTLY) THE LADIES

You are what, twenty? Twenty-one? Twenty-six? Twenty-seven? I just want to tell you right now, that you have no idea how good you look. So just stop with the angst, and the diets, and the fretting. When you are fifty years old you will look at twenty-five-year-old pictures of yourself and wonder why in the world you spent all that time thinking you were fat. You are *so* not fat. When you are fifty, you will see a photograph of the lovely young girl that was you, and you will remember how ugly you thought you were. So run around a little, be healthy, be a good friend and a good person, do thoughtful things for people, be an interesting conversationalist and a good listener, and quit thinking you're fat and hideous. You are gorgeous, honestly. You are in your twenties, and your skin is dewy and supple, and you have energy and the beauty that comes from being young and not yet beaten down. Look at those hands! Look at those nice teeth and that glossy hair. You are a knockout. You need to know that now. So you can stop your whining. Now. Honestly. Go read a book.

STEP AWAY FROM THE COLOGNE

Guys. Easy on the aftershave! I am dead serious. Please. Really, I'm not kidding. I'm not even technically allergic, but certain aftershaves and highly scented deodorants give me that upper sinus headache, the same one you get when trapped in a small elevator with twenty-five elderly perfume-drenched ladies. It starts at the base of the sinuses—I'm not really sure if sinuses have a base, or where exactly the base might be—but the point is, the pain ends up deep in the frontal lobe, and lodges there, and I am staring into the beady red eyes of Mr. Aftershave Migraine. A hug from a scent-saturated gentleman sends me on a slow, forced march into headache hell unless I can immediately hose myself down in the shower.

Generally speaking, aftershave is just a bad, bad idea. I'm telling you because no one else will. It makes people who possess half a sense of smell flee before its overpowering noxiousness. It makes you, an otherwise delightful person, into "that guy who wears too much aftershave." Don't be that guy.

I have a friend who swears that there are wonderful men's colognes out there, and I tend to trust his opinion in all things of the man-realm. He's the go-to guy should you want to know a thing or two about bespoke tailoring, or handmade, French-cuffed oxford shirts, or club ties, or anything concerning the exemplary wardrobing of the discriminating gentleman. I asked this friend for a list of these so-called heavenly man-scents, because I want to believe; I really, really do. I love to wear a good perfume, and a good perfume on a woman can evoke memories, incite daydreams, and be sheer intoxication. But the ham-fisted scents that so many olfactorally misguided men slather on at will tend to render that man more asphyxiating than intoxicating.

My friend insists that a good men's fragrance can even evoke "memories you haven't had." This sounds complicated, but intriguing. So I asked him to send me his list of favorite men's aftershave scents.

Here is his list:

Creed.

My friend says that a good scent can evoke memories you haven't even had.

That was it. One word.

Creed.

Creed is a very old perfume house, founded in England in 1760, now based in France. The kind of place that creates scents using thousands of rare handpicked petals and dew drops gathered at the full moon by virgin maidens, that sort of thing. Creed has created scents for the Empress Eugenie and the Duke of Windsor. Also Cary Grant, Ava Gardner, Marlene Dietrich, and Humphrey Bogart. This is a class joint.

These fragrances are not quite in the same budgetary zone as your Old Spice deodorant stick. But it's time to stop with the Old Spice deodorant stick. No good can come from having your deodorant stick doubling as your cologne. Perhaps you like the retro-kitsch cachet, but do not partake of the Old Spice, as it will cause anyone within a fifteen-yard radius to immediately experience flulike symptoms and upper-eye numbness. It actually burns the inner nostrils. It is the napalm of man-scent.

But there is an alternative to both the dreaded Old Spice deodorant stick and the fancy eau de toilette that could cost you a week's worth of groceries. The trick, if you want to make friends and influence people, is to have a nice shower or bath, and then apply the conveniently *unscented* deodorant you so wisely purchased. Unscented! *Sans* aroma! Absolutely free of bouquet! Devoid of scary man-perfume! If you must slather on something, shake on some baby powder, or sparingly dab— perhaps around the ankle area—one of those single-note essential oils: grapefruit, or coconut, or rain. Then run around a little. Embrace the overtones of guy-smell that emerge with a little sweat. It's free, will not induce headaches in all the nice people you may meet, and it is much more intoxicating than you will ever know.

If You Must Wear After-Shave: Make Your Own! Making your own aftershave is easy, and a much more nostril-friendly alternative to what is in stock at the drugstore and laughingly called "cologne."

You will simply need a small amount of fresh and/or dried herbs, such as lavender, sage, and dried basil.

1. Pack a measuring cup with fresh sage leaves and fresh lavender flowers.
2. Place your mixed cup of herbs into a clean 32-ounce jar, add a couple of tablespoons of dried basil, and pour 2 cups rubbing alcohol OR 2 cups witch hazel mixed with 2 tablespoons apple cider vinegar into the jar over the herbs.
3. Cover the jar tightly, shake for about twenty seconds and let the jar sit for one or two weeks, shaking the jar a few times a day.
4. Strain through a fine strainer or cheesecloth, and apply to your face after shaving.
5. Play around with different ingredients. Try adding some lemon peel, or a few roasted coffee beans, or some fresh or dried peppermint leaves. Dilute with water if the final result proves to be too strong.

If You Can Afford It: Creed. I arrived at my friend's house determined to conduct an unofficial smell test based on his list, and relying solely on my own, biased, admittedly sensitive nose. He is the proud possessor of three Creed scents, so my sampling was cruelly limited, but one random sniff, and I could immediately sense that Creed was of an entirely different order of cologne. It reeked of class and old-world charm, rather than just reeking. There seemed to be layer upon layer of fragrance notes; and whatever the cost of gathering the dew from the eyelashes of musk fairies and handpicking snow-crocus petals, it appears, on first whiff, to be well worth it. I can recommend the following Creed scents, in this order:

* Green Irish Tweed: It's elegant and cheerful, and happily didn't lodge in my frontal lobe. I would consider giving this scent to a very special person. Apparently created for Cary Grant, although Selection Verte is also said to have been created for that icon of debonair charm, in 1955.
* Tabarome: It's got notes of tobacco and something a little sharper. Was told it was created for Humphrey Bogart, so I really wanted to love it, and did love it at first, but it didn't grow on me as much as the Green Irish Tweed.
* Bois de Portugal: Apparently a favorite of Frank Sinatra. Woodsy and musky, reminded me of my grandfather for some reason, but not in an old-guy way. He was a sporty fellow who drank martinis and took luxury liners to Europe.

Now I'm inspired to try all of the Creed scents. I have never liked men's aftershave or cologne, but Creed may have changed my mind. And it has certainly got me thinking about the fragrances created for Marlene Dietrich, and the Empress Eugenie, and that my birthday is coming up. La la la.

Also worth dabbing on: an ingenious man named Christopher Brosius invented the Demeter fragrance line, with such evocative scents as Dirt, Grapefruit, Laundromat, and a personal favorite, Lavender Martini. These delightful perfumes do not hit you over the head or cause those around you to hold articles of clothing up to their faces. Mr. Brosius has a new range of scents in his CB I Hate Perfume line, which are all complex, delicious, and made with no alcohol, only oil and water. And who can resist names such as Mr. Hulot's Holiday, and In The Library?

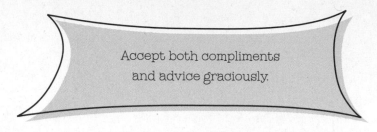

Accept both compliments
and advice graciously.

SEEMINGLY ANACHRONISTIC SKILLS WE ALL SHOULD HAVE: THREAD YOUR SWEATS

You know, the cord on your hoodie? And the cord that holds up your sweatpants? You do the wash and there's the cord, and there are the sweatpants, and they're in two separate places? Well, here's how to reunite them. First, you'll need a safety pin. Do you have a safety pin? Do you know what a safety pin is? Go get a little supply of safety pins, because they are handy to have around. (See page 81.)

Next, simply stick a large safety pin through the end of the cord. This will make it much smoother to drive the cord back through the fabric. Insert the safety pin end into the hole, guiding it through until you reach the other side. Remove the safety pin, and make a good-size knot on each end of the cord.

Some prefer this method: untwist a wire clothes hanger, and tie your cord onto one end of what is now a straight wire stick. Run the wire stick through the casing and it will instantly deliver your cord to the other side. Seems like a lot of trouble to go through, but I suppose once your wire hanger has been untwisted, it might be handy for knocking cobwebs down from the ceiling, and fishing things out of small places.

MORE SEEMINGLY ANACHRONISTIC SKILLS WE ALL SHOULD HAVE: HOW TO TIE A BOW TIE

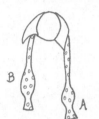

Place bow tie on neck so A hangs down longer than B.

Cross A over B.

Bring A up and under loop.

Double B over itself to form base loop in front.

Loop A over center of loop just formed.

Hold everything in place, double A back on itself, and poke through loop behind tie.

Tug at both ends and straighten center knot. Natty!

(Or ask a bow-tie wearing guy how to do it.)

Go to Brooksbrothers.com to find out how to tie a Windsor, Half-Windsor, four-in-hand, Prince Albert, and Cross Knot.

Should you want to blaze your own fashion trail and go against the conventional necktie establishment, or even if you just want to look like Tucker Carlson for an evening, you'll need to know how to tie a bow tie. All you need is a bow tie, a little practice, a modicum of dexterity, and healthy dose of personal style.

Or simply forget these complicated instructions, and do as a friend suggests: just pretend you are tying your shoes around your neck.

You, in the World, Not Being an Embarrassment

CELL PHONES: JUST STOP IT

And why does your phone look as if it's been surgically attached to your head? Why, oh why are you on it every minute of the day? Are you, like, closing escrow on the Taj Mahal, or making some super-duper important, top-secret deal with the devil? Can't the devil wait for you to get home? Must you be in constant contact with friends and associates while in transit?

Yes, these are rhetorical questions. Right, that means you don't have to answer them. If you have been using a cell phone since you were in your teens, you are probably used to calling your friends, or your mom, to give them a play-by-play commentary on your every move. You might have got used to walking side by side with your best friend while chatting to each other into your cell phones.

No doubt a cell phone is convenient—helpful in emergencies and when trying to find friends in a large crowd. (Especially since most pay phones have been yanked off the streets. What is this "pay phone" of which I speak? Exactly.) But many people have become so reliant on cell phones that it seems they can't be alone with themselves without talking into one of them.

From the time many of you were very young, you've become accustomed to being entertained by some kind of electronic device or other. When you weren't being put in front of a TV, or a computer, or hooked up to an MP3 player, you had playdates arranged for you, and never really got used to entertaining yourself. Perhaps, at this point, you're not quite sure how to face quiet time alone. It could also be that whenever your mother or father got behind the wheel of a car, they started making their phone calls, and now all your friends do it, and you just assume this is what people are supposed to do behind a wheel of a car. I have a friend who calls to chat only when she is driving somewhere in her car. Apparently "watching the road" and "driving" are just too boring to handle without the aid of some stimulating conversation.

Why not give your brain a rest? For one day, try to keep your cell phone turned off, unless you need to use it for some emergency, or for an important work-related conversation. And no, "important work-related conversation" does not mean calling Shannon in marketing to find out how her date turned out.

For one day, rediscover the joy of delayed gratification and anticipation. The anticipation you might feel if you can't talk to someone until you are face-to-face. I am getting all tingly just thinking about it.

Also, and who am I really to say "you look like a crazy person when you walk down the street talking to yourself," but, well, we can't all see that weird earpiece pod that you wear behind your ear so that you will be able to speak to all manner of friend and acquaintance at all times of day. Just so you know, that's why I sort of had that sad look on my face when you walked by. I thought, "Oh, that is so sad! And so young." But it turns out you aren't really a crazy person who talks to himself at all! You just *look* like you are! Oh, I am so relieved!

Safety Tip: If you must use your cellular device, please wait until you have pulled your car over to the side of the road, because just today, as happens every day, more than one incredibly stupid driver did some inexplicable maneuver in front of me and I find that I am still amazed to see that each one of those drivers was holding a cell phone to his ear.

TIPPING

Yes, if you go out to a restaurant, you must tip your waitperson. Waitresses and waiters work hard for a pittance, and you really have to kick in 15 percent for breakfast and lunch, and from 15 to 20 percent for dinner. That's your base, you can go up from there if you're feeling especially flush or generous. If you can't afford to tip, you should wait until you can afford to tip before you go out to dinner. Or get takeout!

ATTENDING A PARTY

So let's say you are invited to someone's house for a big dinner party. I would hope that your first thought would not be, "Cool! Free food!" If that is your first thought, you should keep it to yourself, and exclaim brightly that you would be happy to attend. (If you would not be happy to attend, then you must make a reasonable and believable excuse, and politely decline.)

But let's just say you've accepted. So now you're going to a big dinner party. Cool! Free food!

But in addition to bringing your lovely self, it is also good form to bring your host or hostess a little something upon arrival. A thought-ful host or hostess gift might be a bottle of wine, flowers, or a box of chocolates.

But variations on those themes are allowed, and there are many creative alternatives that might be much more welcome than a box of chocolates. Unless it's really good dark chocolate. Just a hint.

Bring an unusual or at least decent scotch or tequila, if you know your host or hostess collects interesting liquors, or is just, perhaps, an incredible lush. Flowers you have grown yourself, or even tomatoes or lemons from your own garden (if you have them) are a lovely departure from a store-bought bouquet. Or, ask ahead whether it would be help-ful for you to bring dessert to the party.

For instance, I am not much of a dessert maker. I love to cook, but I pretty much always forget about dessert because I selfishly, according to my family, do not possess much of a sweet tooth. (Except for, inex-plicably, little pieces of really good dark chocolate.) Strangely, I would never forget to serve cocktails, or to put out wine with dinner, but des-sert, well, we can't be all things to all people. So if ever a guest calls or e-mails ahead and asks what he can bring, or offers to bring dessert, I often take him up on it, unless it's someone I don't know all that well who is coming over for the first time. You may offer, but if your host or hostess has already figured out the dessert thing, don't insist.

So let's say you've arrived at the party. You've charmed your hostess with a bunch of French lavender from your window box or a single cab-bage rose you have sort of borrowed from your neighbor's front yard. You have talked with friends and have met a few new people and are sipping a cocktail, and you've all just been told to "help yourself" to dinner, a casual affair with various dishes set on a buffet for the gus-tatory delectation of the assembled guests. You are salivating at the stuffed mushrooms, and something with smoked salmon and onions;

you have caught a glimpse of little bite-sized appetizers involving seared Ahi tuna dusted with wasabi caviar. But take a deep breath, and pull yourself together. You will now attempt to make your way toward the buffet table in a dignified manner.

Before you race over to the food, knocking down several partygoers who stand in your way; before you reveal your true, animal nature and start stuffing your mouth to bursting while making faint moaning and growling sounds; before you grab the contents off each serving plate and put it on your own; exercise what little restraint you may still be able to exercise. Grab a plate—and give it to someone else. Avoid cutting in a line that may be forming. Be gracious, and offer to serve someone who might have his hands full. Do not appear to be a person who has not eaten for a full week. Saunter, slowly, without a care in the world, to the food table. Think dignity. Think comportment. Think about others.

Glance appraisingly at the bounty. Know that there *will be enough for you*. Know that you will not leave the party hungry.

In fact, before you serve yourself from the dinner buffet, ask your host or hostess whether you can be of any help. Unless your host has hired caterers and a bartender to take care of the food and drink, peek into the kitchen at some point; offer to help make drinks or bring out a platter of food.

If the party is not a sit-down dinner, and you feel more comfortable sitting with a group of friends than you do joining a group of strangers, that's fine. But if you are able, try to help fuse the separate groups. Be aware if one or two guests don't seem to belong to any group of friends, and invite them to sit with yours. If you are attending a party by yourself, then take the plunge, and sit with a group of people you don't know. Find someone who looks interesting and introduce yourself, if your host has not already done so.

If you are drinking alcohol, drink a tall glass of flat or fizzy water in between drinks, so you don't overimbibe just because you're thirsty. You don't want to make too much of a spectacle of yourself, especially if you're getting to know people for the first time.

If you enter a party secretly thinking people won't like you, or keeping to yourself and a few select friends because you fear the reactions of strangers, just remember that many people may be feeling just as shy or insecure.

If you can just get out of your own head long enough to put yourself in someone else's shoes, you might realize that many people are just as terrified of unfamiliar social situations as you are. Many mask their fear by either being standoffish or drinking copious amounts of alcohol. But if you can help put them at ease, you will be surprised at the response. Sometimes people who seem like aloof jerks are just shy, and the best way to overcome your own shyness is to forget about your own self for a spell, and think about someone else's possible dilemma. (Unless you are just a jerk, in which case, I'm so sorry. Try not to be so much of one, okay?)

Approach strangers with a kind heart and good intentions. Make eye contact, and express interest in them. Ask them questions; people generally like to talk about themselves, and it's a good way to get a conversation going. Don't start in talking about yourself right away, unless asked.

It may be surprising, but within the first five minutes of meeting you, I really don't want to be told the following things:

* How much money you make
* That you read the *Iliad* in the original Greek, and you're surprised I didn't
* That you just bought a very large television set

* How much your large television set cost you
* All about the real estate situation in your neighborhood or town
* Real estate in general
* How much money you hope to be making next year
* That the "fucking asshole" who slapped you with that restraining order still owes you money

If you can't remember any of what I've said, just be a nice person and attempt to enjoy yourself. Try not to drink too much, and know when to leave the party. If at the end of the evening you are surprised to find that you and one other talkative drunk are the only two people left at the party laughing over the remnants of the punch bowl while your hosts busily and pointedly clean up around you, bid a hasty good-night and flee. Perhaps send a nice apologetic thank-you note the next day. Forgive yourself for the occasional lapse. Embarrassment happens. Just try to be more aware the next time you go to a party, and don't let it happen too often.

Just Because It's Good Form: You have been invited to a small dinner party with your significant other. It will be a dinner party consisting of two or three couples, and at some point before you leave for the party, your significant other decides that he or she cannot possibly attend, due to an unexpected work overload, a death in the family, or a plague relapse. At that point, you really should call your host or hostess, and explain in the most apologetic way possible that something unforeseen has cropped up, and how very sorry you are that your partner has to beg off on such short notice. You may think because you are only going to dinner at your friend's apartment that it is "no big deal," but assume that, since your friend has had this dinner party planned for two weeks, your friend has also put a certain amount of care into the planning of the meal. If it was going to be a large party, the absence of

one would hardly be noticeable, but if someone is cooking for four or six, it's only fair to let them know as soon as you possibly can that only one of you will be attending. Surely you knew before you left your own house, and you may even have been clued in quite a bit earlier. A breezy "Oh, Barney couldn't make it" upon arrival might make your host feel slighted, and all the work she put into dinner taken for granted. It may be, in fact, no big deal to your host, but the thoughtful thing to do is to at least pretend that it is a big deal.

EARS ARE OUR FRIENDS!

Be a good listener. You've heard this before, probably as your mother sent you off to kindergarten. "Be a good listener! Use your words!" It is very good advice. Along with pleases, thank-yous, and being able to identify your dessert fork, good listening skills may be the most important social skills you can possess. Listening is actually more important than talking.

Practice on a friend. For instance, the next time your friend tells you a story, try to actually focus on what your friend is saying, as opposed to figuring out what bright thing you are going to say next. Yes, you should attempt to be amusing and clever, but don't hurt yourself. It is so absolutely not amusing to watch someone chuckling over his own jokes, or smiling smugly at how knowledgeable he was. In fact, it makes that person annoying, and ultimately, quite smackable. Don't be the clueless guy by the punch bowl, who no one will go near because he has already dazzled everyone within earshot with such a brilliant display of his wit and knowledge that they all went off to go have some fun. If you find mere mortals too unbearably dull or uninteresting to listen to, then don't attend the party. Go find a nice Mensa get-together, where you can thrill the assembled guests with your insight and wisdom. It's not that most people don't love an interesting conversation full of insight and wisdom, it's just that most people would prefer to not have the wisdom dispensed via monologue, unless they are at the theatre. Listen; talk. Listen; respond. Repeat. That is called a dialogue. That is called a "conversation." Take a breath or two in between sentences. Let other people respond to you. Avoid dominating the conversation. You might actually gain some insight from someone else.

So don't be a crashing bore. On the other hand, the supreme test of politeness is to not show your disdain when faced with a crashing bore. Submit graciously if you find yourself temporarily afflicted with a tedious conversational partner, and if you are seated next to a dullard at dinner, smile, and nod, and be kind. Try not to obviously wince.

Also, if you are a guy, be aware when the women around you are contributing their points of view to a conversation. The tone of the female voice seems to hit the eardrums of certain men in a kind of aural blind spot, and when women speak up to add their opinions to the mix when there is a break in the conversation, it turns out it wasn't really a break in the conversation. It was just the guys taking a breath while gathering their thoughts so they could barrel on through with their next brilliant point.

If, while in the middle of a rousing conversation, you think you hear a small voice attempting to pipe in and make a point, stop. Listen carefully. Search out the source of the disturbance. And allow her to continue, even if you must act as conversational traffic cop.

A NOTE ON BOREDOM

When you are a child, and a teenager, boredom is an entity in your life that must be dealt with. Flailing around the house aimlessly on a rainy and/or summer day claiming to be "bored" is a regular childhood event. Being bored is a way to bond with friends, if you all are bored by the same things. But at some point, as you inch toward your twenties and beyond, you need to listen to yourself finding something boring; it might be time to set aside that particular word, along with your Beanie Babies and Pokemon card collection. Before you make a judgment about something being "boring," you should try to figure out from where that judgment springs, because it usually springs from somewhere just east of obtuse. When you think something is boring, you are merely showing your lack of interest and incurious nature. These are not your best qualities.

When I was in my twenties, I had a dinner party, and over the main course a rousing political discussion began. Afterward, one of my guests sidled up and sniffed that she thought everyone was just "showing off." It annoyed her that smart people were sharing their opinions about world affairs. Now, truly, I do detest a gasbag, but these friends were not at all being gasbaggy, they were just having an interesting conversation. Nonetheless, this friend was bored and annoyed by the whole discussion, because the fact was, she really wasn't up on current affairs, and knew she could add nothing to the conversation.

If she could have just let go of her smothering insecurities for a few moments, she might have allowed herself to be curious; she might have asked some questions, or at the very least been able to sit back and enjoy the discussion. She might have learned something new, and then she *would* have been more informed. Instead of engaging with an unfamiliar group and hearing opinions from people possibly smarter than herself, it made her uncomfortable to feel uninformed. It made her feel like an idiot. *They* were making her feel dumb. They were exposing her ignorance. They were just showing off. You can see how this attitude is kind of self-defeating, and how very self-centered insecurity can be. No one at that table really cared whether or not she was joining in the discussion; no one would have judged her for asking a question.

If I said I think baseball is boring, does that mean that the thousands of people who eagerly watch baseball are all bored to tears? No, they are not. They love baseball. That's why they watch baseball. Consequently baseball can't be boring. Is it boring to me? Yes! Why? For God's sake, what is with the squatting guy in the fencing mask, and the endless standing around!? It just seems like a, well, a big waste of time. Not as much a waste as football, but still, the shortstop, the designated hitter, the bad organ music. Whatever. I know nothing about the magic that apparently takes place between the pitcher and batter. I do not scream at the television with the passion of a thousand white-hot suns when someone for whom I am rooting gets a bad call, and yet, my husband has been known to do that very thing. Would he be moved to yelling at tiny uniformed people in a box if he was watching an incredibly dull game? Is it sheer tedium that drives him to scream "GET OUT! GET OUT! GET OUT!" so that all of our neighbors wonder if he is finally throwing me out on my ear? And why does he howl at the umpire, who clearly cannot hear him? Is it utter ennui? Hmm. Maybe baseball seems boring to me because I know nothing about it. So I really don't have a leg to stand on, when it comes to spouting off my opinions on how boring baseball may or may not be. And if I did start spouting off in such a manner, about how wearying baseball can be, or what a giant bore football seems, then that would be me, being sort of an idiot.

I find math pretty boring; I am not very good at math. Do I know a thing about it? Have I tried to learn? Oh, please. Not since I was forced to, in college. But if someone I know has a passion for math, or physics—or, yes, even baseball—or any number of things I know next to nothing about, I will listen, in hopes that some of their passion—and knowledge—will rub off on me. And in return, I will happily regale anyone within earshot with the little I know about the things for which I am passionate. Shakespeare authorship question, anyone?

Attempt to bring an intellectual curiosity to everything you do. Be interested and open to people and experiences, and you won't ever truly be bored. No one is required to know everything about everything, but intellectual apathy is not a virtue. Don't become so bored that you become incredibly boring yourself.

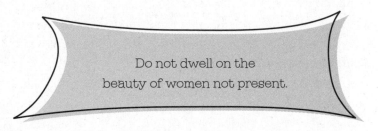

Do not dwell on the beauty of women not present.

This is one of those old saws from an etiquette book. But it's so good, isn't it? Because, I mean, how rude is that? You're standing there, and this guy is going on and on about some woman, who is not you, and how gorgeous she is. Ick.

BE A PERFECT HOUSEGUEST

Should you receive an invitation to someone's house to stay overnight, or for the weekend, you need to know how to behave. If you're going to an exceedingly grand house, the kind of house that keeps servants and wears evening dress for dinner, you are either in a Noël Coward play, or travel in a different circle than I, but your best bet is to be yourself (albeit a very polite, well-mannered version of yourself) and take your cues from your host and/or fellow guests. My knowledge of how to behave in such a setting mostly comes from P. G. Wodehouse and Depression-era movies in which kippers are served for breakfast, liveried footmen announce that "dinner is served," and giant fur collars are featured heavily. There is a better chance that you will be invited to spend a night or weekend with a friend's family, or a friend of your own family, or to meet the family of a girl- or boyfriend, and whether it's a grand house or a modest house, or something in between, you will need to know how to comport yourself with grace. Whether you are visiting the Grand High Sultan of Moneybags, or Mr. Homey Garbage Collector, you must, of course, behave in the same courteous, helpful, and solicitous manner.

It is important to know when to help, when to offer help, and when to simply sit and offer thanks for being so well taken care of. If you arrive, and your host has made a lovely dinner for you, do not eat the meal as if it's the first one you've seen in a month. Alternately, if you are unfamiliar with the food put before you, you must appear to be nothing less than dazzled and delighted, even if the dinner is not entirely to your taste or liking. Unless you are actively allergic to the ingredients, at least taste what's on your plate. If, after a few bites you really, truly can't force it down, move it around your plate a little so it looks as if you ate. You should be familiar with that trick from when you were nine.

When it looks as if everyone is finished, and the host is up and has started to clear dishes from the table, a comment about how delicious the meal was should be followed by the clearing of your own dish, and perhaps the dishes around you, just as I'm sure you were so beautifully taught to do when you were a child.

If you should rise to clear your plate, and your host makes it clear that you should "Sit! Sit!" then you should sit and gracefully accept being fussed over. If you are staying for an entire weekend, or longer, then don't assume that you should sit on your hands every night. If you get up to clear your dishes the second night, and are admonished to "Sit! Sit!" then you must politely insist, in a cheerful way, that you would like to be of help. Try to assess the situation. If your host has a tiny kitchen and seems to be very protective of it, then simply place the cleared plates on a spare surface and ask if there's anything else you can do to help. If it's a large kitchen, and it looks as if your help is welcome, then scrape the dishes, fill the sink with soapy water, and submerge the dishes until you can either wash them or put them in the dishwasher. If your host has the washing thing under control, then offer to dry the dishes. If your hosts really seem to be enjoying your company and if they insist that you not lift a finger, then express your desire to make them a meal during your visit.

It is always best to be helpful when you are staying in someone's house, especially for an extended stay. Keep your room as tidy as possible, even if you've been placed in cramped quarters. Make your bed neatly every morning, as soon as you get up. When you are packing to leave, ask your host if you should strip the bed of the sheets in which you slept. You needn't offer to launder your sheets unless you feel your host would welcome the offer; if a whole houseful of people descended upon the house, your host might want you to leave everything as is and just get out of there as quickly as your feet can carry you. On the other hand, if you're familiar with the washing machine and dryer, your host might be happy to have one less load to do.

Again, try to be aware of your situation, and know when to offer help and when to steer clear. Don't take too literally your host's exhortations to "make yourself at home!" Clean up after yourself, even if you are less than particular in your own house.

Avoid making your "famous pancakes" if it involves leaving the kitchen in such chaos that life is made a living hell for the nice people who invited you to stay. By all means, offer to make dinner or breakfast, but only if you know you can pull it off effortlessly, deliciously, and without causing undo mess and pandemonium. And while making your culinary masterpiece, avoid exclaiming, "Wow, your knives sure are dull!" unless you plan to sharpen them. Don't take over someone else's kitchen unless you can do it cheerfully and discreetly. Ask for the tools you need ahead of time, so you're not frantically hunting down a whisk while your cream sauce boils over.

If your hosts have planned activities, try to be as enthusiastic as possible about those activities. One hopes that they have planned really fun and exciting things for you to do, but if they have invited you to the local library for a Shakespeare authorship lecture and roundtable, you must be gracious. Look happy about it, and you never know, you might have a really good time. You might get all fired up about whether or not Edward DeVere, the seventeenth Earl of Oxford, really is the true author of the works of Shakespeare, and decide to quit your job as a financial planner and get a master's degree in literature. If you honestly, truly, cannot imagine attending whatever it is they have planned, politely beg off, and then quietly figure out how to entertain yourself.

Taking off by yourself from time to time isn't a bad idea if you're staying with someone for longer than a few days. Be thoughtful about giving your hosts some time alone, or at least try to be aware if it seems like they need some time alone.

If your hosts have young children, offer to take them on an outing. Play with them, read books to them, offer to tell them a goodnight story. I guarantee your hosts will invite you back, as free babysitting is better than any hostess gift.

If you can afford to do so, taking your hosts out to dinner is usually appreciated, and will give them a break from cooking. It doesn't have to be a fancy restaurant; maybe you can all go searching for a fun little hole-in-the-wall together. Or combine the above two suggestions, and take their children out for a meal! This will make everyone very, very happy, and shouldn't cost you too much out of pocket, as children don't usually eat truckloads.

And be sure to write a thank-you note when you return home, even if you've already thanked your hosts profusely.

> **Tip:** If you are traveling a great distance to visit someone's country house, beach house, ski chalet, or their house in another city or foreign country, be sure and arrange for your own transportation, including airplane reservations, car rentals, and taxis. Don't assume your hosts will be able to pick you up at the airport, although they may offer. If they insist on picking you up when you arrive, especially if you are arriving at night, or if you're not able to rent a car (the minimum age is usually twenty-five), of course you may graciously accept a ride.

A hostess gift is a nice touch, and if you are under a certain age, it will be most unexpected, and will smooth the path before you, especially if you've been invited for more than a few days. Select a small bouquet of flowers, a box of scented soaps, a bottle of wine—a small token of your appreciation, if you can; and if you can't, just bring your charming, well-mannered self.

DRINKING

Okay, so let's just say you don't drink alcoholic beverages. You can just skip over this next part. But many people do drink alcoholic beverages, and being one of them, I have a few words on the subject. If you are going to do it, now is as good a time as any to develop a strategy, a philosophy, and a sense of style about it. But first, let's start with the cautionary:

The Hangover: Badge of Courage, or Waste of a Day? To entirely prevent a hangover, one could simply not drink, but where's the challenge in that? Then again, avoiding alcohol is the only way to absolutely ensure that you will wake up without the symptoms of a hangover, which may include headache, nausea, and waking up in unfamiliar surroundings—like a Dumpster behind a nameless Vegas motel.

There is a perfectly reasonable explanation why people have been drinking alcohol for thousands of years. It helps grease the sticky wheels of social discourse, it loosens a shy person's inhibitions, and well, whoo-hoo! It's fun. People become chattier, wittier, and generally happier. But drinking is much like plastic surgery; just because a little is good, it doesn't mean a lot more will be better. Because after a few too many, some people don't become wittier and happier, they turn into mean and scary drunks.

It is difficult to assess the effect of a substance on your own brain, when by nature, the job of that substance is to make one lose all professional control. But there are some preventive measures you can take to possibly keep from waking up feeling like death, or worse, opening your bloodshot eyes at daybreak with that nagging feeling that you might have, possibly, done or said something truly mortifying.

For instance, if you do decide to do a little drinking, do not be tempted to start the evening with three martinis and blithely move on to red wine, only to find yourself trading tequila shots with several strangers. This would be a mistake, a mistake you will regret for at least two whole days. The old adage Never Mix, Never Worry is a good one to remember. Also, Mix not the Grape and the Grain. Also, Avoideth the Cheap Red Wine. Seriously. My head hurts just thinking about it.

If you should overimbibe, there is not much you can do, frankly, except go back to bed, place a cool, damp cloth over your eyes, and hope to sleep, interrupted only with occasional whimpering, for forty-eight hours. But there are a few remedies, some of which I will admit to having tried: aspirin, gallons of water, pressing my fingers into my eye sockets and moaning (really works!), a banana washed down with a glass of milk (potassium!), and eating a steaming hot bowl of pho (Vietnamese rice noodle soup, pronounced "fuh," also known as "oh sweet haysoos on a cracker does that taste good") made with loads of chilies. I swear by the oxtail pho.

Eating a hearty meal before you begin drinking heavily is a wise precaution. If you can manage to drink a few large glasses of water and possibly have a banana and some milk before you pass out cold with all your clothes on, you will be ahead of the game when the morning sun hits you like a sixteen-ton Acme anvil. But if all you have is a vague recollection of something involving singing loudly off-key, flirting with a busboy, or telling a relative stranger too much about yourself and/or agreeing to accompany him or her home, I have helpfully included a list of hangover remedies from a variety of sources.

Throughout the ages, drunk and remorseful people have been experimenting out of necessity; and with the help of informal surveys and the magic of Google, I submit to you the following. Try them all! Try them separately, or at the same time! Although I hope you never have to. I cannot vouch for the lot of them, but there seems to be something for everyone:

* Cold, spicy tomato juice or V8. Something in the tomatoes is apparently helpful to the afflicted.
* Pickle juice. I have heard about the pickle juice from many people. The brine from pickles or sauerkraut reportedly works wonders. In fact "raw cabbage" was mentioned, as were "cucumbers," so why not just eat the sauerkraut and a few pickles, washing them down with the brine? A salty snack you can drink!
* Water, water, water. You are more dehydrated than you know. Go. Have another glass. Isn't that better?
* Speaking of water, some hardy—or perhaps desperate—souls swear by swimming in salt water, so a cold dip in the ocean might do the trick. After you have your V8 and pickles.
* A reader of www.thevirtualbar.com recommends two tablespoons of honey followed by several fruit popsicles. Suh-weet!
* A bartender on the same site recommends bitters and soda. Gatorade was a popular cure, and someone else put in a personal plug for Red Bull.
* I think, after all this liquid, you are going to need a little food. Protein is a must, so go boil an egg. Eat it slowly. Or crack a raw egg into a blended banana and milk shake.
* Alka-Seltzer Extra Strength seems to be a perennial favorite.
* Menudo. No, really. A bowl of steaming, hot entrails. In a lovely, spicy broth. Hungry?
* Two tablespoons evening primrose oil. I can't remember who told me, but it couldn't hurt. Take it by capsule, along with 250 to 500 milligrams of vitamin B12. Then dab some of the evening primrose oil under those baggy eyes.

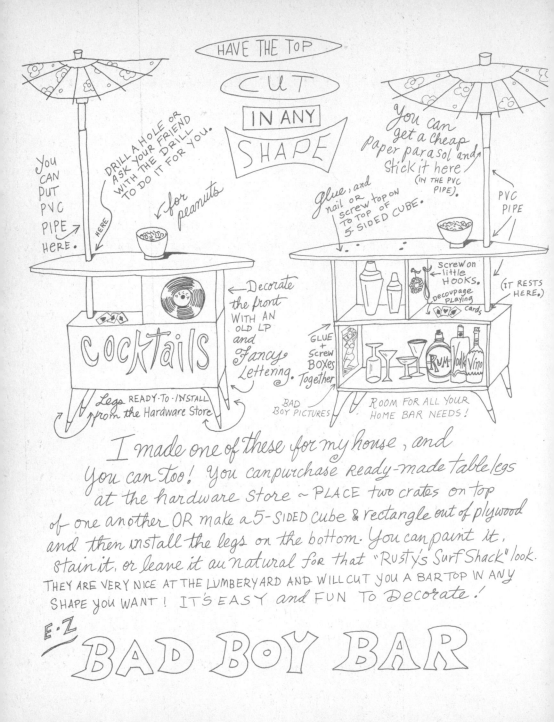

HAVE THE TOP

CUT

IN ANY

SHAPE

YOU CAN PUT PVC PIPE HERE.

DRILL A HOLE OR ASK YOUR FRIEND WITH THE DRILL TO DO IT FOR YOU.

HERE

for peanuts

You can get a cheap paper parasol and stick it here (IN THE PVC PIPE).

PVC PIPE

(IT RESTS HERE.)

Glue, and nail or screw top on to top of 5-SIDED CUBE.

Screw on little HOOKS.

decoupage playing cards

← Decorate the front WITH AN OLD LP and Fancy Lettering.

COCKTAILS

GLUE + Screw BOXES Together

BAD BOY PICTURES

RUM Vodka Vino

ROOM FOR ALL YOUR HOME BAR NEEDS!

Legs READY-TO-INSTALL from the Hardware Store

I made one of these for my house, and
You can too! You can purchase Ready-made table legs
at the hardware store ~ PLACE two crates on top
of one another OR make a 5-SIDED cube & rectangle out of plywood
and then install the legs on the bottom. You can paint it,
stain it, or leave it au natural for that "Rusty's Surf Shack" look.
THEY ARE VERY NICE AT THE LUMBERYARD AND WILL CUT YOU A BAR TOP IN ANY
SHAPE YOU WANT! IT'S EASY and FUN TO Decorate!

E·Z
BAD BOY BAR

* Did I say water, water, water? Please, go have another glass. I cannot stress this enough.
* Do not take ibuprofen before you drink alcohol thinking that you will circumvent that headachey feeling. When combined with alcohol, it will wreak havoc on your liver, and there is not one party worth years of dialysis.
* Airborne and Emergen-C, both high in vitamin C and zinc stuff.

Now, obviously, "eating a hearty meal before you drink heavily" and some of my other useful suggestions should not be considered advice for healthful living. It really isn't very good for you to drink to excess, as it will kill many brain cells, make you eat too much, and assist you in doing things the thought of which will either make you blush, or want to move south of the border and live out your days in seclusion.

The fact of drinking could simply be ignored, much like thinking that if we don't tell teenagers anything about sex except to not have it, they will not have sex. Ha! Of course drinking should be done only occasionally, and in moderation. But the road to hell is paved with good intentions, and eventually you might overindulge. And when that happens, make sure you drink plenty of water, try to be with good friends, and whatever you do, don't get behind the wheel of a car, because that would be stupid and dangerous.

And if you decide that you like to partake of an alcoholic beverage from time to time, well then, learn to do it properly, and with style. Be a good host, keep your bar stocked, and be prepared, so that you can spontaneously ask people over for cocktails and nonalcoholic beverages alike. Being able to throw a small party at a moment's notice is welcoming and hospitable. Not to mention fun.

Remember This Important Tip: Tossing your cookies, upchucking, worshipping the porcelain god are all an unpleasant and unfortunate side effect of drinking too much alcohol, just your body's way of saving you from possible death by alcohol poisoning. But, if you vomit in someone's car, or if you throw up while you are with a group of friends, those friends will remember your throwing up long after you have forgotten. You may, in fact, have no recollection of the incident the next day. But twenty years from now, when those same friends picture you, guess what they will picture you doing?

Oh, What the Hell! Where's My Cocktail Dress?

IT'S YOUR TURN: HOW TO THROW A REAL GROWN-UP COCKTAIL PARTY

Rather than having just a regular party, the kind where you basically call up a bunch of friends and say, "Hey, uh, wanna come over Friday night? Sure, bring some beer! Awright!" why not have a real cocktail party? It doesn't have to be a formal affair, but a cocktail party is a little less haphazard than calling up a handful of random friends, who call some other friends, and then everybody just, like, shows up when they feel like it. A cocktail party is when you compose some sort of guest list, and sort of actually plan the party. And they always seem better when they aren't too, too big.

Think about who might like to meet whom, or who might mingle well with other friends of yours. Perhaps there is a person at work you want to get to know better; a smallish cocktail party is a great way to integrate newer friends with friends you have known a long time.

Introduce your friends to one another. It is amazing how many people do not do this, but if a friend of yours arrives who doesn't know a soul, it is your job to take the new arrival around to friends who have already arrived, and introduce him or her.

Every sociable, grown-up person should have a home "bar," whether it's a cupboard devoted to a few beverages to serve your guests, or a garage-sale tiki bar fully stocked with every mixer under the sun.

Even if you are not a drinker of alcoholic beverages, you can still be a thoughtful and genial host by keeping an assortment of alcoholic and nonalcoholic beverages with which to ply your guests. Your fairly low-budget starter kit might include:

* A six-pack of small club soda bottles
* A six-pack of tonic water
* Fizzy waters or interesting retro soda pops
* Frozen limeade, orange juice, and lemonade (to keep in your freezer)

Keep an assortment of beer on hand, which you can purchase as your funds allow. And when you can financially manage it, buy a bottle or two of decent wine. You can collect enough for a smallish "wine cellar" (which can go in a box under a table, or in a cool closet; lay the bottles on their sides to keep the cork moist) so that you will always be ready when friends come over—or if you need a bottle at the last minute to bring to someone else's house.

Vodka, gin, tequila, scotch, and bourbon are optional, depending on how much you or your friends like mixed cocktails. But if you do, you will need to stock your cupboard with a jar or two of olives—stuffed with pimento, garlic, or jalapeño—and a jar of maraschino cherries, the kind marinating in a liquid the color of which is not found in nature. A little box of toothpicks could come in handy, as would a set of tiny paper umbrellas or those little monkeys that hang on the sides of large

The Basic Bar : Glassware

Cocktail

margarita

Collins

Old-Fashioned

Beer PILSNER

manhattan

Brandy Snifter

Bloody Mary

Whiskey

Champagne FLUTE

blue beverages at tiki bars. And you don't even have to buy them, just remember to bring them home after a night at a bar, and ask your friends to collect them for you, too.

If your fridge doesn't have an icemaker, little plastic ice cube trays can be had at any supermarket. And you can find basic glasses for your bar from thrift shops (mismatched glasses are adorable) or a culinary supply house, in bulk; maybe a friend will go in on a bulk box of martini glasses with you.

A cocktail party is less about the alcohol than about the attitude. Getting a group of interesting friends together is much more interesting when everyone remains fairly coherent, so make sure you keep a bottle of fizzy and flat water available, so that your guests don't just keep drinking alcohol because they're thirsty.

THE MIGHTY MARTINI: DON'T MESS WITH PERFECTION

What could be simpler, yet more sublime, than a martini? There's not much to it: gin and a dash of vermouth. Shake over ice (or stir, if you buy that nonsense about "bruising" the gin) and serve in a chilled, stemmed cocktail glass. And yet, the beauty of its simplicity eludes most mortals.

It has happened once or twice that an acquaintance will come to my house, and exclaim that he or she has never had a martini, and gee, they've always wanted to try one, and golly, could I make them a "light" one? There is no such thing as a "light" martini. It does not exist in nature. You either have a martini, or you don't have a martini. And if you have reached a certain age without ever having had one, I suggest you stick with something less potent, possibly something fruity poured over crushed ice, sporting a tiny umbrella. Then there will be more martini for me.

Various hipster eateries and watering holes about town all seem to have the ubiquitous "martini menu." Somebody out there thinks that if you put any old kind of swill in a triangular, stemmed cocktail glass and call it a martini, then it *is* a martini. These people are sadly misinformed. For instance, I could chill a cocktail glass, pour into it a splash of club soda, and call it a "virgin martini," but that would be silly. I could take a chilled cocktail glass and pour some milk of magnesia into it and call it a Johnson & Johnson Martini. But that would be disgusting. Anyone would say, and rightly so, "That's not a martini, that's milk of magnesia! Who the heck do you think you are kidding with that?" Likewise, when someone mixes up cloying, sour-apple-flavored corn syrup with two ounces of vodka and calls it a martini, I get very, very sad. First of all, if you want a "vodka martini," then order a vodka martini, but that's another story. If you want a sour-apple-flavored concoction, then give it a kicky name of its own, and do not confuse the issue, or try to lend this abomination some kind of ersatz class by calling it a martini. One can put a diamond tiara on a pug and call it "Princess," but no one will confuse it with actual royalty. I should think that if these drink inventors have the misguided imagination to come up with such a vile potion, they should have the respect and decency to name it something appropriate. Perhaps a Gumdrops 'N' Lollipops, or Green Apple Gagger, or Oh Lord I Am Going to Be Sick Tomorrow.

Do not keep your gin in the freezer. Freezing your vodka is a nice idea, especially if it's decent vodka, and you want to pretend you're in St. Petersburg in January while you toss it back without a lot of fussy mixers. If you will be adding a lot of fussy mixers, then keep your cheap vodka frozen as well, because it will make it taste better.

Freezing your gin just makes it thick and gelatinous, and decidedly unsuitable for mixing a martini.

I once gave an acquaintance my recipe for a perfect martini, and soon after I was invited to her house for cocktails. Being aware of my proud reputation as an alcohol aficionado, and specifically a martini drinker, she thought she would try her hand at martini making. She apparently thought it would be a lot of "fun," sort of like the first time you inject vodka into a watermelon, or try making fresh margaritas from kumquats. I was immediately suspicious of her enthusiasm. She seemed all too excited about serving martinis—a sign that it was a novelty and not a time-honored tradition, a sign that martinis were not in her blood.

With sorority-girl zeal, she opened the freezer and proudly revealed a cocktail shaker, which she assured me had been placed there "the night before"—meaning that the night before, she had placed a cocktail shaker full of gin and a splash of vermouth, into the freezer.

She pulled out oversize cocktail glasses and proceeded to pour thick, slushy, frozen gin into our glasses, looking at me all the while with a conspiratorial glint in her eyes as if we were wild, young things from an Evelyn Waugh novel, drinking bathtub spirits. I searched for the words, so that I might politely tell her she had forgotten one very important step in the mixing of cocktails, and that would be the "mixing" part. Something along the lines of "Oops! You forgot to shake it over ice!"

You see, something magical happens when the gin and vermouth get shaken with the ice and strained through it. The sophisticated roué about town, gin, meets a rustic, warm, Italian vermouth. They kiss, briefly; they are shaken; they are stirred. But I held my wincing and my bad analogies in check, and a few minutes later sweetly asked for a glass of ice water, wherein I surreptitiously fished a few ice cubes out, plopped them into my cocktail glass and swished them around quickly before tossing them out. No one was the wiser. Don't give me any nonsense about not wanting to "water down" your martini, either. Trust me, shaking your gin martini over lots of ice is necessary. Do it in a cocktail shaker before you pour the drinks, to avoid embarrassment.

And speaking of oversize glasses, martinis are no more meant to

be served in giant cocktail glasses than they are meant to be served in fishbowls. Giant, stemmed cocktail glasses are meant for margaritas, and cosmopolitans, and drinks embellished with fruit and foam. An elegant, stemmed cocktail glass is a much better choice for a martini. And if there is a "dividend" left from mixing the martini, save it in one of those little chemist bottles, or a small tumbler, and serve it alongside the martini. Chill your glasses ahead of time; serve a martini with an olive and a Gibson with a cocktail onion. Cheers!

MORE DRINKS

A Really Easy Fake-Tropical Rum Drink: I first had this drink at my friend Rosina's house, so I think it's her recipe. It is an exceptionally easy way to make an impressive rum drink when you just don't have the time to whip up a homemade simple syrup or hand squeeze the juice from ninety-two limes. Thank you, Rosina!

SOME ABSURDLY EASY HORS D'OEUVRES

It's a good thing to keep a variety of food stocked at home, not only for your own health and well-being, but in case you should discover you are entertaining friends unexpectedly. If a group of friends pop over, or even if you have planned for an invited party of guests, you really shouldn't break out the alcoholic beverages without offering your guests some food.

There are a handful of food items that can be stored in the cupboard for those evenings when some bright person suggests that everyone go back to your place to continue the evening. Keep bags of raw almonds on hand for a healthful snack for yourself; when guests arrive, roast

An Extremely Easy Fake Tropical drink

Rosina's LIME Rumba

2 Tablespoons Frozen Limeade
2 oz. RUM
Club Soda
Mint and Sliced Limes for garnish

Scoop a couple of tablespoons of the frozen
limeade into a tall glass. Add two ounces of
rum, and mix together. Fill the glass with ice,
add the mint, if you have it, and muddle into
the ice. Top off with club soda. Stir gently,
and garnish with a slice of lime. If you don't
have mint or lime, trust me, no one will care.
A little paper umbrella would be a nice touch,
if you want to go that extra mile.

them on a cookie sheet with olive oil and spices for a delicious Spanish appetizer that goes with any kind of drink (see page 125). If there is a particular kind of cheese that you like, for instance, keep two packages on hand. That way if your friends never come over, or you don't have any friends, it will eventually get eaten and won't go to waste.

I like goat cheese, and I know that it keeps in the fridge for a few weeks at a time; so I keep it around, and when friends come over for a glass of wine I put the goat cheese out on a nice plastic Scooby Doo plate, pour some olive oil over it, and grind some black pepper over the top. They actually sell logs of goat cheese with the ground pepper conveniently sprinkled on top, but, hello? Save a dollar and grind your own pepper for two cents. Crackers or bread may be served alongside. If you don't have any crackers or bread on hand, let's hope you have some cheddar, or another hard cheese lying around without too much mold on it. Just cut some up into little cubes and serve. You can put toothpicks in the cubes, for a very fancy touch. Better than a sock in the eye, right?

Jars of artichoke hearts are good to keep around; cut them in pieces and arrange them next to the cubed cheese. And peanuts. I mean, come on, how hard are peanuts to keep around the house? And cheap! Buy them roasted in the shell (if you can find them, and if you're entertaining outside) to give your guests something to do with their hands. Keep a few jars of olives, or in a pinch, even the canned black olives with the big holes will do. Your friends will have lots of fun putting them on the ends of their fingers and eating them off, just like when you were all seven years old.

ROASTED SPICED ALMONDS

2 cups whole blanched almonds (although I've used almonds with skins to
   delicious effect)
1/2 teaspoon cayenne
1/2 teaspoon paprika
1 teaspoon cumin
3 tablespoons olive oil
1 tablespoon coarse salt

Preheat the oven to 300°F. Toss the almonds with the spices and olive oil and place in a single layer on a foil-covered baking sheet or a large cast-iron pan. Roast the almonds until golden brown, 15 to 20 minutes. Allow to cool a little before serving. Have a handful. And that is why you need to keep a bag or two of raw almonds around at all times.

THE SMOKING AND DRINKING THING

Just keep those little habits in check, is all I'm saying. Because what may look incredibly cool when you're fresh faced and hip doesn't look the same when you're older, and those little vertical lines are etched into your upper lip, and you're hunkered over a cold chardonnay at 10:00 AM. You don't want to become so attached to your vices that you can't put them down anytime you want.

If you aren't a smoker, and if you don't drink alcohol to excess, then I'll give you a couple of Brownie buttons to go with your Ovaltine. Perhaps you have some other faults, and your friends aren't too annoyed by your perfection because you can drive them home. But your friends should know that there is nothing more depressing than walking past one of those "smoking sections" you see at various ballparks and arenas. It is like they gathered together the most desperately sad, grayest people they could find, and put them together under a cloud of smoke. It is so far removed from cool it is staggering. It is as cool as rickets.

Also, there is a very fine line between the charmingly tipsy and the you-are-such-a-sad-old-drunk, and you really don't want to lose sight of that line. If you didn't die of alcohol poisoning in college, then bravo, because a stupid amount of young people die of alcohol poisoning in college. So take advantage of your live state, and don't become an extreme boozer and smoker.

Really cute twenty-two-year-olds can get away with slurring their words and becoming incoherent after four cocktails. It's kind of adorable. You know how bad they'll feel tomorrow, and, although you don't want to be there to hold their cute twenty-two-year-old heads above the toilet, you won't hold it against them if you have to. The thing is, you can get away with an awful lot of excessive drinking in your twenties, and your body bounces right back. It seemingly bounces right back because our bodies are amazing machines and it is their job to set about the business of healing. Head cold, bullet wound, or hangover, it is all the same to your body, which just starts working overtime to get you better. But you want it to be able to do this for a very, very long time, and if you start taxing it with too many injudicious nights out, it will get back at you when you are forty-five, by making you look like you're sixty-five and feel like you're a hundred.

I know, right now you're thinking, "forty-five?" and sort of snickering into your sleeve, like that's going to happen. Well, it will, if you're lucky. And when those happy golden days do arrive, you don't want to be one of those cheerless, old drinky people with the watery eyes that look as if they can't wait for their next drink, even while they're in the middle of their first one.

Put on Those Big Boy Pants!

HOW TO THROW A REAL GROWN-UP DINNER PARTY

A buffet is a fine solution if you know you don't have chairs enough or place settings enough for a really large group, but let's say you want to try a sit-down dinner party for six or eight, or even ten.

First of all, your plates don't have to match, and your glasses don't have to match. You shouldn't keep yourself from having a dinner party just because you think you should wait until you have a complete set of Limoges, or twelve matching, lead crystal wine glasses.

There is no right or wrong way to throw a dinner party. They are all variations of: make dinner and invite friends over to eat it.

The conventional dinner party serves cocktails and a perhaps a few small appetizers first, to give everyone a chance to arrive. A variation on that theme is to invite friends for dinner at seven. Tell them to be on time. Serve dinner at seven fifteen, and have your cocktails and other beverages after dinner, so you can all hang out without having to feed everyone in the middle of the party.

The most important thing about having a dinner party is not to make

How to Set a Table: An Illustrated Guide

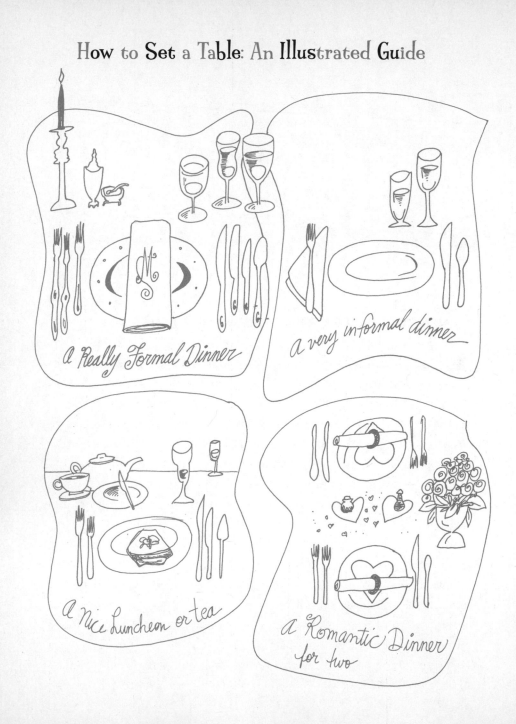

A Really Formal Dinner

A very informal dinner

A Nice Luncheon or tea

A Romantic Dinner for two

A Buffet Dinner

Dinner Alone on a Saturday Night

Dinner alone on a Saturday Night with your dog

it so formal or complicated that you don't have fun at your own party. It's supposed to be fun for everyone, not just your guests. Presumably you like the people you have invited to your residence, and want to celebrate them with a delightful dining experience. You want to enjoy their company over food and drink. You cannot do that if you are stuck in the kitchen sweating over guinea hens in puff pastry, braised asparagus, and steamed egg custard with shaved truffles ramekins. Your guests will hear you whimpering, and they will feel bad, and they'll wish you had all just ordered pizza.

If you love to cook, really love it, and your friends are game for you to try out new and exotic dishes on them, then by all means tackle whatever kind of meal you are in the mood to tackle. But if you want to make things easy, look for dishes you can make the day or evening before. Slow-cooked stews are very forgiving and very homey. Serving a cold dinner is an easy way to entertain (cold poached salmon! cold chicken salad!), and if you're having a crowd you can always make a large vat of chili (along with a small vat of vegetarian chili, as a thoughtful gesture), which usually makes everyone happy.

Always have enough to drink. Always ask your guests if there is anything they need. It would be thoughtful to have a pitcher of water, or a bottle of bubbly water out within easy reach, so thirsty guests can help themselves.

It's always a good idea to ask your guests well ahead of the big event whether they have specific food allergies or if there's anything they just don't eat. Most vegetarians will insist that you not make a special dinner around their needs, but if I know those needs ahead of time, it might help me plan a menu that will be enjoyed by everyone. If you find that a friend is suddenly "wheat sensitive," or feels that onions make her "bloat," or is just finishing up a monthlong "cleansing fast," you are not required to make her a separate dinner.

Even if the actual "dinner" part of the dinner party consists of nothing more than peanuts and pizza, make a little production of it. Use the nicest plates you have, or if you don't have any nice plates, give your party a picnic theme. Then the paper plates, plastic checkered tablecloth, and plastic utensils are suddenly all part of a well-thought-out plan. Eat on blankets that have been carelessly strewn about the room; wrap your utensils up in paper napkins tied with raffia, or something. If your food isn't the main draw, at least make it look as if you put some energy into making a party.

WHAT THE HELL AM I SUPPOSED TO DO WITH THESE FLOWERS, ANYWAY?

Bringing flowers to a party is a wonderful way to thank your host or hostess, and a fine alternative to bringing wine or chocolate.

So, let's say a guest has been so thoughtful as to bring you a large bouquet of flowers, while you are in the middle of preparing for a party. How nice! How considerate. They are so pretty. Now, um, what do I do with them?

Yes, dumping the flowers in a vase of water is an option, and if you don't have five minutes to fuss with them, that is exactly what you should do. But if you do have five minutes to fuss, fill up a vase with water, then fill your kitchen sink with a little water as well. Roses especially like to have their heads soaked in water, but most flowers that have been rolled up in butcher paper for hours would benefit from some moisture.

The trick to make flowers last is simple: clean your stems so that there are no leaves in the water, which creates stinky bacteria-laden water that will make your flowers die and make your dining room smell

There really is
no right or wrong
way to arrange

flowers.

THEY
ARE
FLOWERS.
I mean
HOW BAD can
flowers look?
You really have
to WORK
AT IT
to make a hideous flower arrangement.

(BUT IT
CAN BE
DONE.)

you can mix flowers with fruit. You dont have to use vases. you can
make it look as if you went on a walk use unusual containers, buckets,
and picked a bunch of flowers flowerpots, and old boots lined with plastic.
and stuck them in a handy vase.

like an old peat bog. Make sure you always scrub or soak your vases with hot water and a few drops of bleach to kill the flower-killing bacteria. And cut your stems, preferably underwater, before placing them into your vase. Figure out how short you want the stems to be by holding each flower up against the vase and eyeballing it.

So, have a clean vase standing by, clean your stems of their lower leaves, cut your stems on an angle underwater, and place your flowers into the nice, clean vase. Easy.

There is no need to use a "frog" or "oasis," both of which support your flowers when making Ichibana arrangements in shallow dishes or wide-mouthed vases. Sometimes the nicest arrangements are those that don't look too arranged at all. Try making little groupings of interesting vases with just a few flowers of the same type in each vase, which often look much more eye-catching than one big huge vase full of mixed flowers.

The best flower arrangements, to my mind, are the ones that look as if they were just plucked from the garden and haphazardly stuck in a jar. So, for that kind of un-arrangement, place the greens or the leafier flowers into your vase first, to make a base in which you can artfully arrange the main flowers of your arrangement. The leafy filler will help support the flowers in the vase, if you don't have a huge amount of blooms.

You may have received some lovely tulips, or mums, or tuberose, which really are very nice on their own; but some enthusiastic florist felt the need to randomly add a wad of baby's breath, or an armful of leatherleaf fern or lemon-leaf branches. Do not feel obligated to jam the whole thing into your arrangement. The ubiquitous lemon leaf and leatherleaf fern can sometimes add a much-needed green element to a bunch of flowers, but please use both sparingly. Baby's breath, on the other hand, isn't actually grown in real people's gardens, and tends to mark your arrangement as having arrived straight from the florist. Baby's breath is kind of pretty on its own, but has an oddly cheapening effect the minute it's paired with almost any flower, even very expensive ones—*especially* very expensive ones. Pairing baby's breath with a bunch of giant peonies would be like hanging black velvet paintings in the Taj Mahal, or putting lipstick on a baby, or upholstering a Corbusier in pleather. So, lose the baby's breath. Unless you love baby's breath, then fine. Just do me a favor and put it in a separate vase. In the bathroom.

That said, if a friend brought me a bunch of baby's breath wrapped in newspaper, I would think it the sweetest gesture in the world. I would be in raptures over such a delicate and delightful bouquet. I would adore it. Am I insane, or merely pretending? Neither. I wouldn't be pretending at all, unless my friend owned a florist shop and it looked as if he fished the baby's breath out of the Dumpster before bringing it over. But if a poor art student living frugally fished that baby's breath out of the florist's Dumpster, now that would be thoughtful, and genius. Does that make sense yet? Flowers are a thoughtful gift to bring to someone, but they needn't be an expensive bunch from a florist, is what I'm trying to say. You could pick some daisies by the side of the road, and your host or hostess would be very pleased and think you the nicest person at the party. Even more thoughtful is to arrange the flowers ahead of time, in order to save your host the bother of having to arrange flowers while attempting to make beverages for arriving guests. The vessel you choose needn't be extravagant. Anything that holds water will work beautifully, even carrying the flowers with their stems in a plastic bag filled with water and tied up with elastic, the way we used to carry goldfish home.

MAKING YOUR OWN HOSTESS GIFT

If you have a little time during the afternoon of the party, and you'd like to exert more creativity than is involved in the buying of a bunch of plastic-wrapped double freesia, you can make a very interesting arrangement in the comfort and privacy of your own home. You can cut some small branches from a tree in your backyard, or a neighbor's yard, or from a tree or shrub in a nearby park. Use these branches as the base, and with the addition of ordinary household items or things you may have lying around, you will delight and astound the recipient with a wildly unusual and creative arrangement.

Here's what else you'll need, and how to do it:

1. A container of your choosing. This can be an old cookie tin, a bucket, a vase you'd like to give as a gift, a wooden crate, an old boot, whatever.
2. One or two pieces of floral oasis, available at any florist or craft shop.
3. Three, five, or seven branches; large, small, or a mixture. Think odd numbers, because it is more pleasing to the eye. And it really is.
4. A utility knife. Some garden clippers might be helpful, too.
5. Green moss, or Spanish moss, or even a piece of fabric (this is to mask the oasis).
6. A few floral water tubes (optional).
7. Dental floss, fishing line, or fine wire.
8. Any goofy little plastic bauble you have lying around. Little hula ladies? Plastic fish? For a pittance, you can get packages of cowboys and Indians or plastic dinosaurs from the crap aisle

at your local drugstore. Or get one of those bad Barbie knock-offs, or get three. (Odd numbers!) Or use some old postcards, or if you have some beads you can string, or a deck of playing cards! The point is, what looks like a bunch of junk that is collecting dust in your apartment will be transformed into a treasure once it's used to make this fabulous arrangement.

9. Hot glue might come in handy, but if you don't already have a hot-glue gun, don't go to any trouble.

So, let's get started! I presume you have found your container. Good, I really didn't want to have to come over there and find one myself.

Cut your floral oasis to fit the container. If you are going to be using fresh flowers or branches with blossoms, soak the oasis in water first, letters up. If you are using dried branches, you don't have to soak the oasis. If you're using an old cookie tin, you'll probably need both oasis rectangles. If you'll be using an old boot, you can just shove the oasis in on its end. (Line the boot with plastic first, if you're using a waterlogged oasis.) Anyway, you'll figure it out. Just make sure the oasis is jammed in there nice and snug.

Next, take your branches and whittle down the fat ends until they're pointed and smooth, and free of all knobby, pokey things. Stick your branches into the oasis, preferably in an artful manner. For instance, the fattest or largest could be stuck in the center, straight up, to act as the anchor, and smaller ones could branch out from the bigger one on either side. But figure out where you want to stick in the branch and then leave it there. Once you've jammed something in an oasis, you can't keep pulling it out and repositioning it, or the oasis will disintegrate.

Now you've got your base built. If you want to keep it very simple and Japanese-y, you can, at this point, stick a single, gorgeous bloom of some beautiful flower into your floral glass tube, or directly into your wet oasis. Three smaller flowers will do as well. (A giant garden rose? Three dahlias? Cut the flowers underwater at an angle, fill the glass tube with water, then insert the flower.) Place the single flower or three smaller blossoms at the base of the branches.

Take your Spanish moss, or your green moss, or your fabric, and bunch it around the base of the branches, to mask the fact that you have just stuck some branches into a green floral oasis. Poke in a couple of straight pins, or a piece of wire at an angle, to anchor the moss or fabric. If you really want to get snappy, place an interesting rock, or piece of wood at a rakish angle at the base of the branches. Or get three interestingly shaped rocks and paint them in bright acrylic colors.

If you want to inject some humor into your gift, or if you don't have the budget for any fresh flowers (or your own garden), this is where your plastic hula girls, fish, or playing cards come in. Tie your dental floss or fishing line, or wrap a length of wire around whatever object you have chosen to decorate your branches. Hang the various objects from the branches in a decorative way. Use your imagination, for heaven's sake. You could hang playing cards from the branches, and glue little dice around the base. Miniature toy cars would be a delightful addition.

If you want to go a little more floral, fill a bunch more water tubes with blossoms, and tie them with ribbons to your branches. Or paint your branches in fuchsia pink enamel or fire-engine red, and keep your decoration minimal.

Decorating Tip: A collection of anything, even used—I mean "vintage"—hairbrushes, looks cool by the mere fact that it's in a "collection." I have no idea why that is. One old, plastic baby-doll head with ratty hair just looks sad, but put ten plastic baby-doll heads together arranged on a shelf, and you have a really cool collection. Arrange them in a glass case, and you have a cunning art installation. If you have a bunch of single socks that have lost their mates somewhere in the single sock ether, collect them, mount, and frame them behind glass. Call it "Lost Socks." Hang it on the wall. Whoa! Art!

A WORD ABOUT CARNATIONS

They're not so bad! People got all sniffy about carnations several years back, and their reputation has never quite recovered. But they really are sweet, and affordable. In the olden days they were called "pinks," which I love.

Yes, it's true, for the longest time carnations were a staple of the tackiest flower shops, a cheap way to add filler to an inexpensive arrangement. And those large red carnations do have that assembly line, manufactured look about them. But put a giant bunch of those little double carnations in a really cool vintage vase, and the result will be elegant and retro. Even the awful red ones have a certain air of jolie laide, especially if you put them in the goofy, dreadful vase you found at that garage sale. It's always good to have a few ugly vases around for humorous flower arrangements. Unusual soda bottles make wonderful vases; line up three on a table with a single carnation coming out of each one.

Also, although I abhor the sickly looking St. Paddy's Day green carnations, if one did have a little hankering for a bunch of blue, or purple, or orange carnations, you can make your carnations edged in blue, or purple, or orange. If you never undertook this fascinating experiment in third grade, or should you need your memory jogged, here is how you do it: Get a bunch of white carnations, add the food coloring of choice to some water that you have poured into a container or vase, cut your carnation's stems, and plunge. They will suck the dye up through their stems, and in the morning you will be the proud owner of some carnations sporting hues not usually found in nature.

HAVE A PICNIC!

You don't have to pack a fancy picnic hamper with cut glass and linen napkins to have a good picnic, although it can be fun to make a picnic extra swanky. But a picnic can be very simple, too; you can make peanut butter and jelly sandwiches, or throw in a baguette and some cheese. Deviled eggs are a classic picnic food, but even plain, old hard-boiled eggs with salt and pepper are easy and portable. Throw in something to drink, and maybe a bottle of water if you'll be walking in addition to picnicking, and you've got a picnic. You'll want napkins, utensils if necessary, and a blanket, or some kind of ground cover. If you live in the city, take your picnic to a city park, spread out your blanket, unpack your picnic and a few books, and settle in for a leisurely afternoon. If you live in the suburbs, see if you can walk somewhere other than a shopping mall. Look for somewhere with trees. If you live in a rural area, you may already be a regular picnicker, so good for you. People just aren't having enough picnics, and I think we need to bring them back.

The Holidays: Starting Your Own Traditions

It can be a tricky thing, knowing when to assert your autonomy when it comes to The Holidays. It is always nice to spend holidays with your mom and dad and siblings, if you are lucky enough to have parents and siblings whose company you generally enjoy, especially if the feeling is mutual. But now you are settled in your own place, possibly with a roommate or roommates. You have a group of friends, many of whom are separated from their families by great distances. You, in fact, may be separated from your own family by a great distance, and at some point you decide you are going to start your own holiday traditions. It usually starts with Thanksgiving.

Thanksgiving is a holiday that adapts very well to all variations and types of families. It is a very forgiving holiday. It is about eating, and friends, and eating with friends, and cooking, and eating some more. It can be about family, but if you live away from your parents' house, you might start taking in all of your stray friends who have nowhere else to go, and you might just decide to all have a big potluck feast because honestly, at this point, your friends are your family.

Thanksgiving is about turkey, but you don't even have to eat turkey. You can have a themed dinner, where everybody brings a dish from seventeenth-century Massachusetts, or a favorite Thanksgiving dish their mother used to make, or a Native American Thanksgiving dish, or even a meal composed of authentically awful Thanksgiving food—the ubiquitous marshmallow-topped canned yams, or those sad, overcooked Brussels sprouts that Aunt Elyse used to bring. Or just delegate, and have everyone bring whatever it is they like to make the best. Just make sure you don't end up with twelve bags of store-bought dinner rolls.

Know the strengths and weaknesses of your guests, and don't make anyone cook who doesn't really like to cook. If someone doesn't like to cook, they can bring some wine, or the dinner rolls.

Think of what you liked to eat for Thanksgiving dinner when you were growing up. I happened to love the celery root salad that my mother made, but I am not in any way representative of most people. I also know the words to obscure Annette Hanshaw songs and the plot lines of Shirley Temple movies. In reality, most people want the turkey, the gravy, the stuffing, and the mashed potatoes. They only put the rest of the stuff on their plate to be polite. Really, if they could, they would just pour gravy all over themselves and bury their heads in the stuffing dish. So make sure you make triple the gravy that you think you will need. Hey! Why don't I give you a recipe for really, really good gravy?! Because even if the bird is totally dried out and your stuffing sucks, you can pour a bunch of this gravy over everything and it won't matter.

GRAVY, I MEAN, OH, GOOD GOD, GRAVY

What really makes this gravy a great gravy is that I make my own turkey stock, and lots of it. Using a lot of sherry, incidentally. Normally, a person would take the neck out of that little packet that is hiding inside the turkey's body cavity, clip the ends off the wings and use that to make stock. But the superior gravy maker buys two or three extra turkey necks, and adds those (with the above trifles that come with your turkey) to a large heated stockpot, into which you have thrown in a little olive oil. Brown the necks and wing tips, then add two carrots chopped into large pieces, a bay leaf, a quartered onion (with the skin left on to color the stock), a few pieces of celery, a handful of whole garlic cloves, a few sprigs of fresh dill, and five whole peppercorns.

When everything gets nice and browned, add one cup apple juice, one cup sherry, and two of those quart cartons of organic chicken broth, scraping up all the browned bits on the bottom of the stockpot. Top off with water, if necessary, to cover the stuff in the pot. Cut one lemon in half and squeeze the juice into the pot; throw in both lemon halves. Add a handful of thyme sprigs and several leaves of sage. Keep the pot on a medium-low simmer for two to four hours, adding more broth or water as needed. Another cup of sherry wouldn't hurt. You want to end up with at least eight cups of stock, so that you can use a few cups in your stuffing, and the rest for your gravy.

After three hours or so, remove the large pieces of neck and vegetable, and strain the rest through a sieve into another pot. Let cool, and refrigerate. It is much easier to make the stock a day or two ahead of time, rather than doing it all on Thanksgiving Day. After chilling it overnight, you can skim the fat right off the top, keep it hot on a back burner, and use it for your various needs the day of the big feast.

OH, GOOD GOD, GRAVY

8 tablespoons turkey fat (skimmed off your chilled turkey stock or from
the turkey juices from your fat separator)

8 tablespoons flour

8 cups strained turkey stock

1/2 cup sherry, if desired

Salt, to taste

1/2 cup heavy cream (optional)

A whisk and a fat separator would be helpful.

1. Just before your turkey is ready to take out of the oven, heat up
the lovely turkey stock you made a day or two before. Remove
your turkey from the oven and place it on a large cutting board.
The kind with a trench, so that turkey juices won't start drip-
ping off the cutting board onto your counter and floor, right
when you're in the middle of making the gravy. Trust me. You
want the trench. (Your turkey should rest for about twenty
minutes before you eat it anyway, so that will give you enough
time to make your gravy. Take this opportunity to remove all
stuffing and traces of stuffing from the turkey cavity, so your
guests don't fall ill before the pumpkin pie is served.)

2. Pour the turkey drippings—which is all the juicy stuff left in
the turkey roasting pot—into your fat separator, and wait for
the juices to magically sink to the bottom. It won't take long.
Skim 8 tablespoons of the turkey fat off the top of the fat separator (or use the turkey fat you have skimmed from your stock),

and put them into the turkey-roasting pan, which still has all the browned bits and stuff stuck to the bottom. Turn the heat on low. Whisk in the flour until it gets a little browned; then slowly add the hot stock, whisking adamantly all the while.

3. Add the 1/2 cup of sherry, slowly, if you like. Your gravy should be nice and thick, but not gluey. Taste it. Does it need a little salt? If so, whisk some in. Some people like to chop up the giblets and add them to the gravy. I do not. Sometimes I will add mushrooms that I have sautéed with a few dashes of freshly ground nutmeg. If you want a very rich gravy, add a 1/2 cup of heavy cream. Keep the burner on very, very low to keep the gravy warm while you are slicing the turkey. Serve! Eat! Marvel! And accept compliments graciously.

Tip for the Lazy Cook: Use one of those mesh poultry-stuffing socks for stuffing your turkey. You put your turkey dressing in the sock, stuff it into the turkey cavity and cook your turkey. When it comes time to remove the stuffing you just pull out the sock, and with it comes all that juicy stuffing, leaving behind no bits that might cause the growth of weird turkey bacteria.

TOOLS

For God's Sake, Do I Really Need a Fat Separator?

A fat separator, or gravy separator, is a glass pitcher-type container that is used to separate the fat from the juices of the meat. The juices from the roasted turkey (or any roasted meat containing fat) are poured into the separator; the fat rises to the top, while the juices miraculously

a fat separator— sometimes called a GRAVY separator

a wire whisk

remain on the bottom in a lovely layer of meat juice. The spout that extends down to the bottom where the juices are located allow them to be poured out while the fat remains on the top, making it easy to separate the two. If you don't use one, your gravy could be kind of greasy. I'm just saying.

A Wire Whisk

A wire whisk is good to have around for a lot of reasons, especially when making your roux, which is the fat-and-flour thickening mixture for the gravy. Also, when the hot stock is added to the roux, the whisk is the best tool for preventing lumps.

Whisks are also helpful for scrambling eggs, mixing French toast batter, and whipping cream without an electric mixer.

OH, PLEASE: THANKSGIVING EDITION

If you've been invited to a friend's house for Thanksgiving dinner, and you know that your friend is making a sit-down dinner for twelve, try not to call a few hours before you arrive and ask to "bring a friend." Or a couple of friends.

Even worse is saying that you have another Thanksgiving dinner to attend, and that you can stay only for a little while.

Even worse is having the friends you brought say that they can stay for only a little while, because they have another Thanksgiving party to go to.

And try never, ever, if you can help it, to ask your hostess the day before or the morning of Thanksgiving if you can bring a friend because your friend is going through a nasty breakup and is having a really hard time, and has nowhere to go, especially if your friend shows up, eats a hearty plate of food, and leaves before dessert because he has "another Thanksgiving dinner to eat!"

First of all—and this goes for all parties, not just Thanksgiving—when you stop by someone's party on your way to another party, you seem to imply to your host that much more fun is to be had elsewhere, that anywhere else would be more fun than where you are—and that you'll be off to enjoy all this fun as soon as you've had a little bite to eat. You might as well be telling your charming hostess that her party is a mere stopover on the way to the real party. "Too bad you're not invited!" is the unspoken subtext. "Enjoy your lame partay, loser!" Perhaps you think I am laying it on a little thick. But honestly, it is just the rudest thing. If you'd rather be somewhere else, then go there first. And stay there. And don't imagine that you're missing some great party when you don't come to mine. I'm sure mine will be very dull, and the food will be bad. Or maybe it won't. You'll never know. La la la la la.

These party hoppers are generally the same people who, when you are having a conversation with them at a party, tend to look past you to whoever has just arrived, or whoever is passing by. You know these people. It is exceedingly irritating to have conversations with them, as they always seem to be searching for someone more interesting than you with whom they can converse. So, don't be that person, either.

Am I taking away all your options? Who can you be? What is left for you? How about, don't be the asshole! Don't be the irritating jackass. Don't be that shallow, thoughtless, and ultimately rude person who still believes that the world was designed to cater solely to his care, feeding, and pleasure.

Of course there are exceptions. If you are stopping by an early cocktail party on your way to a late dinner party, then that is perfectly acceptable. Or if you are required to go to a business function that was scheduled the same night as your friend's party, well then by all means stop by your friend's party, letting her know how much you'd wish you could stay, before heading on to the office bash. And if you are just not feeling up to staying late at a party, well, of course it's okay to leave early. Your host will understand. Unless you are heading off to another party.

The grass is not always greener, and sometimes where you are is where you are supposed to be.

WHY THANKSGIVING IS THE BEST HOLIDAY EVER

Once you have started your own Thanksgiving tradition, you come to the realization that this is the best holiday ever. True, there is no rotund, bearded gentleman sneaking down the chimney to bring you gifts, but a lack of gifts also means that you are not required to get a bunch of gifts for other people, either. What you get is the gift of eating great food with great friends; at least that is the goal.

Everyone seems to have grown up with a slightly different Thanks-giving tradition, and if you ask around you will find people getting all nostalgic about their family's Thanksgiving lasagna, or the annual Thanksgiving macaroni and cheese. Just as some people stuff their turkeys with oysters and others with sausage, you, too, can make your Thanksgiving meal an instant tradition by deciding on a dish to serve and sticking to it, year after year. Years ago Calvin Trillin suggested spaghetti carbonara as being a better choice than turkey for Thanks-giving, something Columbus may have taught the Native American's ancestors years before. But come on, we all know by now that Colum-bus was just another lost sailor, and that America was really found five hundred years earlier by Leif Ericsson, a Nordic-Icelandic guy. And probably years before that by the Polynesians.

So why not a Norwegian-Icelandic feast, or a Polynesian luau on Thanksgiving? Or make a token colonial dish that might have been served at the first Thanksgiving celebrations, like succotash. Or some Native American dishes, or if you are intent on honoring Columbus, paella! He sailed from Spain, after all. If you prefer meatloaf to turkey, how about a meatloaf shaped like a turkey? Ask all your friends to bring their lasagnas, their macaroni and cheeses, their marshmallow-topped yams, their favorite Thanksgiving dishes—the comforting foods with-out which Thanksgiving would not be Thanksgiving.

My Mom's Celery Root Salad: One of the most delicious dishes ever. If you have never had celery root, it has a flavor faintly redolent of celery and artichokes, and is scrumptious shredded raw, or lightly steamed, as in this recipe. I'm sure my mom's version was found in some 1950s cookbook, because you don't see much Green Goddess dressing on anything anymore, and that's a shame.

So, go foraging for a couple of celery roots. Celery root is pretty much available in most grocery stores these days. If you can't find it where you live, grow it, or move to a bigger city. Or to France, where they really know how to eat.

Rinse and peel the thick, knotty skin off the celery root, and cut it into one-inch chunks. Plunge the celery root pieces into a bowl of water into which you have squeezed the juice of a lemon, so it won't get brown.

Put about an inch of salted water or vegetable broth into a pot and bring to a boil. Throw in the celery root, cover, and cook, testing at about five or six minutes. You want the celery root to be firm but not crunchy, and certainly not mushy. You'll figure it out. If you can stick a fork in it, it's done. It's pretty forgiving, just try not to overcook it. When it's done, remove it from the heat and put it in a bowl to cool.

Now the Green Goddess dressing. When the celery root is cooled off a bit, pour the Green Goddess dressing over it, toss, and chill for at least an hour or so, or all day while you cook the turkey. Green Goddess dressing is also an excellent accompaniment to fresh romaine leaves, avocado, cucumbers, coleslaw, artichokes, and just about any crunchy, watery raw vegetable you can think of, although it will smother and overpower baby lettuces. It also goes well with cold, poached salmon, shrimp, crab salad, and grilled fish. Experiment!

A Note to Those of You Who Are Weird About Anchovies: If I didn't tell you there were anchovies in Green Goddess dressing, you would never know. You would only wonder what in the world gave the dressing that piquant and lively taste, and you would beg me for the recipe. So, trust me on this, put in the anchovies. Mash them up and you won't even know they're there, and neither will your friends who are weird about anchovies. It'll be our little secret.

GREEN GODDESS DRESSING

1 cup mayonnaise

1/2 cup sour cream

1/4 cup whipping cream

4 green onions, chopped

2 tablespoons chopped garlic

1/3 cup fresh chopped parsley

4 flat anchovy fillets

2 tablespoons fresh chopped tarragon

1/4 teaspoon salt

1/4 teaspoon freshly ground white pepper

Combine all ingredients in blender or mixer and puree. It will keep up to three days in the fridge.

HOW TO MAKE YOUR OWN CHRISTMAS TREE

Follow the instructions for "Making Your Own Hostess Gift," but make everything bigger. (Unless you want a really small tabletop tree.) Make your base a giant bucket or washtub, and get some long curly willow from your local flower mart or cut some branches from your neighbor's tree. Your neighbor may appreciate the pruning, but do ask first. You can paint the branches gold or white, or you may even spray on some of that weird white flocking for an added bit of kitschy elegance—or leave them in their rustic state, for a little bit of the outdoors in your living room.

Make your Own Christmas Tree!

If the branches are especially heavy, find some big rocks or pieces of broken brick and place them in the container to stabilize the branches at their base. If you want something a little more permanent, mix up some cement and pour it into the container once you have your branches set the way you want them. Hang ribbons, fake flowers, playing cards, Buddhist prayers on little scraps of paper, or even the traditional colorful, breakable Christmas orb. Hang whatever you would like to hang on your Christmas tree. It's your Christmas tree. Have a party and invite friends to bring an ornament to hang on your tree. Then if you decide to have a traditional green tree next year, you will have all the ornaments given to you by friends.

A Note on Christmas Trees: At my house, a Mexican puta doll is our Christmas tree angel. For many years, when I couldn't afford to buy "real" Christmas ornaments, old rhinestone glasses frames, loteria cards, and other assorted junk stood in for the real thing. But then I realized that I already *did* have the real thing, and that all those knickknacks festooning my tree all those years *are* real Christmas ornaments. Yes, Virginia, even that crappy plastic bride and groom, and the Christmas Elmo someone gave me, and that giant fake pink flower! I had the most specialest ornaments under my nose the whole time!

LET'S CELEBRATE BAD ORNAMENTS WITH SOME EGG NOG!

1 dozen eggs, yolks separated from whites

1/2 teaspoon salt

2 1/4 cups sugar

4 cups bourbon (Optional, use more or less as you wish.)

1 cup rum (Optional, but come on, it's egg nog! But okay, fine, use more or less as you wish.)

5 cups whole milk (2% milk is acceptable—add another 2 cups milk if
  you're not using alcohol.)
2 tablespoons vanilla extract
5 cups heavy cream
Nutmeg, freshly grated if possible

1. In a large mixing bowl, beat together the egg yolks and salt,
   slowly adding 1 1/2 cups of the sugar. Continue beating until
   thick and pale.
2. Stir in the bourbon, rum, milk, and vanilla until well mixed.
3. In another bowl, beat the egg whites until foamy. Slowly add the
   remaining 3/4 cup sugar, continuing to beat the egg whites until
   they've formed peaks and all the sugar has been incorporated.
4. In a third bowl, whip the cream until soft peaks are formed.
   Fold the egg whites into the yolk mixture and then fold in the
   whipped cream, and a good dash of freshly grated nutmeg.
   Taste and add more bourbon and/or sugar if necessary.
5. Chill for a few hours, then pour into a punch bowl, grating
   more nutmeg on top. (You may set the punch bowl in a bed
   of ice to help keep it chilled.) Makes about 24 servings, so if
   you're having a small party, you can halve the recipe. Unless
   you all want to drink a lot of egg nog. Cheers!

Astro Weenie Christmas Tree

Go to YouTube, and search for Astro Weenie Christmas Tree. There
you will find the little film of Charles Phoenix assembling this remark-
able space-age holiday confection, the Astro Weenie Christmas Tree.
You can make one, too! Charles will show you how easy it is to throw
one of these babies together in time for your next holiday party.

Q-Tip Snowflakes!

Mexican Lottery Cards

La Serena

RECYCLED ORNAMENTS!

Cardboard Cereal Boxes cut into Shapes

THE FOLLOWING ITEMS WERE USED TO DECORATE MY HUSBAND'S CHRISTMAS TREE WHEN HE WAS IN HIS TWENTIES

Q-tips

Dental floss (draped like tinsel!)

Baseball cards (not the valuable ones)

Post-Its

Cassette tapes

Kazoos

Reminder from Kindergarten: You can make the Q-tips into snowflakes! Arrange three Q-tips into a snowflake/star shape. Tie in the middle with some dental floss, tying off the dental floss ends so that the ends make a loop. Voila!

Money-Saving Christmas Tree Buying Tip: If you don't need a fabulously huge and expensive tree for a party you're throwing in early December, I have often found that making the rounds of the Christmas tree purveyors a few days before Christmas will get you a much better price. If you can wait until Christmas Eve, the price should drop even further, especially if you look as if you really need a break on the price. Bring some homemade Christmas cookies to those guys at the lot, it's cold out there!

If you don't want to pay a dime for a tree, but you'd like to have a tree when you entertain, then plan your holiday party for *after* Christmas. Because the day after Christmas you will start seeing Christmas trees on the street, in alleys, and dumped into bins. You should have a fairly extensive choice.

If you break a glass or a Christmas tree ball, use a dry cotton ball to pick up the smallest little bits of broken glass. The cotton fibers catch ones you can't see! (It is ridiculous how much stuff like this my friend Geri knows.)

NEW YEAR'S EVE: THE GREATEST
PARTY OF THE YEAR! NO PRESSURE AT ALL!

Is there anything worse than a New Year's Eve party? The forced gaiety, the self-conscious milling about. It's New Year's Eve, the last party of the year, the first party of the year, THE BIGGEST PARTY OF THE YEAR, and you are expected to have the time of your life. It's the ultimate Saturday night, and it's enough to make you want to crawl under the covers until Groundhog Day.

I love parties. I adore a good excuse—or any excuse—to get dressed up in fancy togs. I love the food, the revelry, seeing friends, and meeting people. I love to see everyone all sparkly and dressed up and parading around with their party hats on, eating canapés and being charming. I am definitely pro-party—on every other night of the year, that is, but New Year's Eve. It's just too obvious, or something. You know? Honestly, people feel like they *have* to go a party on New Year's Eve, and so they do, and they end up standing around with people they don't know very well, and if you don't have a date, you wonder if anyone will kiss you at midnight, and if you do have a date, it is somehow way too meaningful if you kiss your date at midnight, and if you have a very special date, you really would rather be elsewhere with that person. It's a lose/lose situation. So why not lower your expectations, as I do?

Every year, I fill the table with foods I love to eat, stock up on something I like to drink, and let my friends know that if they'd like to drop by, I would love to have them. But it is *not* a party. If they are looking for a New Year's Eve party, they should avoid my house—no, no party here. Ix-nay on the arty-pay; Yes, festive foods will be available, some sort of sparkling beverage will be on ice, I will probably have a fire going in the fireplace, and music will be playing. Two friends might come over, or five. Some friends might stop by for a few hours on their way to a Big Fabulous New Year's Party, to which I say, "Have fun! Buh-bye!" Some friends might come for an hour and end up staying until 3:00 AM, and everyone who stays is required to sing "Auld Lang Syne" (with ukulele accompaniment) when we call our friends and leave singing messages on various phone machines. It is kind of totally sappy, but we've been doing it for years, and it's so much fun. One year we serenaded the telephone operators. They were very understanding.

I basically have a quiet evening at home, except a little louder, and usually with music. I celebrate with no expectations. And I always have fun, because it's always a little bit of a surprise.

So create your own New Year's Eve rituals, which will soon become your own New Year's Eve traditions. If the pressure to Have Fun is just too much, get together with a few like-minded friends and have a New Year's Eve Triple Feature night, or New Year's Eve Chess Marathon, or New Year's Eve Beach Run. If you really want to have a big party, have it the following weekend, when everyone doesn't have another party to attend, and they can all come to yours.

SOME THINGS TO DO ON NEW YEAR'S DAY

If you don't have a calendar of some sort, here is a good reason to start keeping one. On New Year's Day—or New Year's Eve, if you are having a *really* quiet evening at home—get your calendar off your desk, or off the wall, and put it next to your new calendar. As you start transferring all of your friend's birthdays from your old calendar to your new one, you can review the year, one month at a time. It's kind of fun, and will

bring you little memories, like of the day you met Lisa at the museum for the photography exhibit, or when you all took your friend Max to the sumo wrestling match for his birthday, or the reading you went to at that little independent bookstore downtown, or the midnight movies where you fell asleep.

Affairs of the Heart

BREAKING UP IS HARD TO DO

Yes, breaking up is hard, but imagine how hard it is on your friends, especially if you have broken up and gotten back together with the same person twenty-seven times in the last year.

Have you ever been involved vicariously in a good friend's romantic entanglements? Let's say your friend breaks up with her boyfriend because of some egregious bit of behavior on his part; out of loyalty to your friend, you decide to hate the ex-boyfriend, too. You hate him so much! Bolstered by your long-standing friendship, you hate your friend's ex with a blazing, seething passion. You bad-mouth the ex-boyfriend, you trash the ex-boyfriend, you assure your friend that you always hated him, and that she is so much better off without him. Then, just as she seems to be pulling herself out of her funk, she and the ex-boyfriend get back together. Great! You dissed him in the street when you ran into him, you told your friend that you had always distrusted him, and you told everybody you thought he was an asshole. But now your friend has made her choice, and she has chosen the ex-boyfriend. If you want your relationship with your friend to continue, you have to hope they both have short attention spans or very generous natures.

Some couples thrive on breaking up, and they break up on a regular basis, sometimes over the course of many years. Sometimes the high drama can be seductive, and sort of fun—the late-night phone calls, the dramatic reconciliations, the broken crockery. But if you sense that a friend's romantic relationship has taken a turn for the high drama and somehow you have become involved in the tearful phone calls and the breaking up every other week, and should you find yourself in too many conversations that go on, and on, and on—about whether he really loves her, until your eyes are crossed and you want to throw her new kitten out the window—the smartest strategy is to stay far, far away. Extricate yourself from the center of your friend's love tornado. Step away from the spectacle and move yourself to a noncommittal, neutral position. If you un-involve yourself from the situation, or at least make it clear to your friend that you find the whole production silly, your friend either will have to listen to you or find another friend to support her personal passion play. If your friend is really a good friend, he or she will come back to you after the dust has cleared.

I had a friend who started dating another friend of mine. Eventually—probably owing either to heavy drinking or to some misfired synapses that caused a series of inexplicable errors in thinking—they moved in together. She was known to say, often after the fourth breakup of the month with this boyfriend, "He *said* he doesn't love me, but I know he doesn't really mean it." Hello? Um, if someone told you to your face, "I don't love you. I have never loved you," wouldn't you just want to leave quietly in the dead of night out of sheer embarrassment? Yet my friend seemed to think that true happiness could only be hers with someone who really didn't like her all that much. Oh, sure, her boyfriend liked having sex with her, and he liked that he had a place to live practically rent free, and he liked the fact that she cooked dinners for him, and he liked that he had a working fridge for his beer. He thought she was really, really *nice*! But in those biweekly flashes of genuine honestly, it was clear that he did not feel they were a match.

She insisted that he must have been just kidding, and so, based on little more than her delusions and the fact that he was living pretty comfortably, they dragged out their personal misery another year or two until she finally scraped enough of herself up off the bottom of his shoe to call it quits.

And by the way, what is wrong with the following sentence? "I had a friend who started dating another friend of mine"? Never, ever, introduce a really good male friend to a really good female friend and encourage them to date. Don't "set up" good friends of yours. If they choose to start seeing each other romantically on the sly, and it all works out, then you can laugh about it later. But you had better hope it all works out, or you are bound to lose one of them as a friend if the fur starts to fly.

JUST A THOUGHT . . .

* Thinking about going out with your friend's ex? Oh no you are not.
* Do not suddenly become really good pals with your friend's ex, unless you were friends with him or her first.
* Do not suddenly start having coffee with your friend's ex so that your friend can pass information to the ex through you and/or gain information about their ex from you. Do not get sucked into the middle of their mutual drama society. Surely you can find some real friends.
* What about those pictures of you and your ex where you look really good? You want to save the photograph, but you just don't want any reminders of that relationship. Tip: Do not cut out the head of your ex, or in any way mutilate the photograph. There's

nothing that says to the new person in your life, "Hi! I'm a psycho!" more than a bunch of photos with gouged-out faces. Digitize them, run them through some Photoshop-type program, and gently remove the offending party. Put the originals away in a drawer or a shoebox to show to your kids in twenty years, by which time you will have presumably gotten over your old flame.

THE UPSIDE OF BEING SINGLE AND LONELY!

So, you've been dumped by your girlfriend, or you have dumped your girlfriend, or you and your boyfriend parted very amicably, or you and your boyfriend decided to end the relationship, with or without an enormous amount of pain. You're sad it's over, or maybe you feel a sense of relief. Maybe you're despondent, depressed, and playing a lot of music about how somebody done somebody else "wrong." But two days later you have that restless feeling, and you're ready to get back on that horse.

Can't be without a boyfriend or girlfriend for more than two days at a time? Maybe you aren't really lonely, maybe you're just bored. With yourself. Yes, a constant stream of companions can help you avoid ever having to be with yourself, but it will also help you avoid ever getting to know yourself very well. And if you never really get to know yourself, how are you going to find a partner who will finally be right for you?

"But," you say, "I do know myself, and I know that I like to be in a relationship! What's wrong with that? Shut up."

Of course it is natural to want an intimate relationship. Having a companion can be nurturing, challenging, and very satisfying. But there are many upsides to being alone with your own bad self for a while.

* Self-sufficiency. You will figure out how to take care of stuff on your own, without depending on your big strong boyfriend to take care of everything for you. You *can* patch that cracked wall! You *can* empty the garbage!

* You will learn to cook for yourself without expecting your domestically inclined girlfriend to make every meal for you.

* You will have to clean up your own mess, but on the other hand, it's your own mess, not someone else's.

* You get to decorate your apartment any way you want to decorate it. What, your girlfriends don't think that giant inflatable beer bottle is adorable? Come on! Blow it up! It's yours! And I think it looks just wonderful next to the mantel, where you have hung your Godzilla poster.

* You can find out what it is you really like to do with your time, without the influence of another personality.

* Extra time in your day will not be devoted to pleasing another person.

* You will have time to take an interesting class on the weekends.

* You will have time to read some good books, or catch up on the classics, which will make you a more fascinating person.

* You'll have more free time to be really, really sad.

* In fact, you will have enough time to really wallow in your sadness.

* Plus extra time to revel in your loneliness.

* You can listen to any kind of music you want to listen to, and you can turn it up really loud. You might even discover you have totally different taste in music than you thought you did.

* Also, you can secretly gloat when you notice couples you know bickering over really stupid stuff, or when you see your friends

having to do things they don't really want to do, because their girlfriend or boyfriend *wants* them to.

✳ You can take a break from worrying if that skirt makes you look "too fat."

✳ You can get in touch with your own creativity; write, paint, draw, sing, learn to play an instrument, or get better at playing an instrument you already know how to play. These are things best done alone and when you start getting really good at any one of the above, you will start enjoying spending more time by yourself. And if you get really good at playing an instrument, you can eventually find some interesting musicians to hang out with.

YOUR PERFECT IMAGINARY PARTNER

I have a friend who used to be single. She didn't want to be single, and she was not happy as a single person, although my secret feeling was that it wasn't her single status that was making her unhappy; she just wasn't happy. A relationship was not going to help her be happier with herself.

In any event, this friend of mine used to have a list, an actual list that she made, a list that listed the must-have qualities of the boyfriend/partner/eventual husband for whom she would be willing to settle.

The list was specific, and rather extensive. This amazing imaginary person had to possess so many sterling qualities that my husband and I both wanted to find him ourselves and marry him. What a catch! She didn't think her list was asking too much, in fact she only put down the qualities she felt were the most important to her. And why not?

There is nothing wrong with yearning for a partner who is graced with a good sense of humor, or one who has a job, or is not a Republican. As long as you don't make the list too long, and as long as you really don't expect to find someone with every quality listed. And as long as you don't make your list so unrealistic as to assure a solitary life, unless that's what you want.

I am all for lists. I am pro-list. Lists are good things to make, in general, and a list will certainly help you get a clear idea of what you are looking for, or what you are not looking for. Maybe you will find someone with every single wonderful trait you put down on that list; stranger things have happened. But if you are so determined not to settle for anything less than:

1. Over six feet tall
2. Not blonde!
3. Outdoorsy
4. Passionate about politics
5. Great cook
6. Witty
7. Romantic!!!!!
8. Loves to garden
9. Carpentry skills
10. Keeps the house clean
11. Enjoys going to theatre
12. Great sense of humor
13. Must know how to sail
14. Good speller
15. SMART
16. Knits and sews

17. Likes to cuddle
18. Loves to travel!
19. Musical talent/plays instrument
20. LOVES BOOKS
21. Really good job
22. Owns his own house
23. Adventurous
24. Good writer
25. Knowledge of foreign policy
26. Lifts weights with me!!
27. Bakes
28. Has tattoos (Japanese)
29. Rides a Moto Guzzi Falcone (pre-1958)
30. Speaks fluent French (and Spanish?!)
31. Will go bicycle touring in Europe with me
32. Can plan a vacation
33. Can arrange flowers
34. Willing to live on a boat with me for a year

. . . then perhaps you are not really looking for a boyfriend, but rather a handyman, a maid, girlfriend, librarian, chef, gardener, exercise partner, personal concert pianist, Proust, Popeye, and George Clooney.

Often such lists are made based on our previous romantic experiences, and because of our previous experiences, we have become acutely aware of the things we will no longer accept in a potential mate. That can be a good thing, if "no more racist junkies!" is on the list, or "must be literate." But if you start putting down "no magicians!" or "curly hair only," you might miss out on some really interesting straight-haired magicians. And they can be a lot of fun, seriously. Especially when they do the close-up stuff, with the cards. I am a total sucker for that stuff.

The point is, you are not going to find one person who can be all things. If you like to go hiking, and your boyfriend doesn't, well then, you can go hiking with your other friends who do like to hike. If you are a professional hiker, and it is the most important thing in your life, then you will probably want to find someone who shares similar interests, so go ahead and look for your dream hiker. Just be open to all possibilities. Our mates don't have to share our every interest; that's why we have friends.

Some guys make lists, but the only ones I know who make a really stringent mental tally of acceptable and unacceptable qualities that they must have in a potential girlfriend (blonde, tits, looks like a model, gotta be HOTTTT!!!), often don't have very lasting relationships and generally think women are "bitches."

But what many guys are looking for are not what many women *think* they're looking for, and vice versa.

"Women just want a guy who makes a lot of money" is the one I hear the most. And some women actually think, "Men only want tall, gorgeous model types with giant breasts." Well, some men do, but think about it for a minute; are those the guys you really want to be hanging out with? Because when you talk to those guys, they kind of look at your chest a lot, which is kind of creepy, and they aren't generally very bright. Regular nice guys sometimes have a mental list, too, but the lists usually aren't very long. The most basic wish I heard was something along the lines of "Yeah, I want to be attracted to her, but if she makes me laugh, then I'll follow her to the ends of the Earth." The more complicated lists included:

1. No squeaky voices
2. Not a psycho
3. Interesting face
4. Doesn't get all defensive when you disagree
5. Has interests outside the relationship
6. More well-read than I am
7. More interested in planning things than I am
8. More romantic than I am
9. Likes to clean more than I do

Okay, so he's a little lazy, and wants her to take the initiative to do practically everything plus clean up after him. But on the other hand, he's not being utterly unrealistic; the list seems reasonable. And who doesn't want someone to clean up after them? A lot of the guys I spoke with don't need a partner to be all things. They don't need her to love sports, just because they love sports. If she does love sports, then fine. But by and large, it seems a lot of guys want someone whom they find attractive, who isn't deranged, who has a sense of humor, and who likes them back. End of list! That's a nice general list that everyone can use. The point is, be receptive. Don't make your lists so specific that your choices for a Saturday night date become narrowed down to an inflatable party doll and a bag of microwaveable popcorn.

DON'T GIVE YOURSELF A HAIRCUT
WHEN YOU'RE DEPRESSED

I know when you're crying on the sofa in your ratty bathrobe with a bag of popcorn watching *Roman Holiday* that the temptation is great to pull out those little scissors and snip away at your head. Audrey Hepburn

OOPS.

Self-Inflicted
Bad haircuts
Due to broken hearts.

looked adorable, after all, with her chic Italian haircut and those short little bangs. And when all is said and done, it's only hair, and it *will* grow back. Eventually. Just understand, before you start in with the scissors or straight razor, that hair doesn't grow back overnight. It actually takes much longer than you might think.

It is common for people in a recently broken-up state to want to alter their appearance in some way; you are starting fresh, you are reinventing yourself. If he liked your straight strawberry-blonde hair, miniskirts, and leopard mules, well just about now you may feel like transforming yourself with a short, platinum gamine cut, black capri pants, and ballet flats. If she always preferred your mousy brown hair in a neat, corporate do, you might just want to wake up tomorrow with a black mohawk, and start growing an indigo soul patch.

I am all for experimentation, and I think it's healthy for young men and women to experiment with their looks. Life is too short to go the safe khaki route, and I would just hate it if you found yourself thirty years hence scanning the racks for the "relaxed fit" of the same style of Dockers you bought for Casual Friday thirty years before. Tiny Audrey Hepburn bangs are an excellent look to give yourself at least once, and if you have always pined for golden locks or hair the hue of red crayons or deepest mahogany, then what is hair for if not to dye?

But you might want to wait until you're not wracked with grief over an unsuccessful romance before practicing your artistry on your own head. The same advice goes for tattoos, and getting an obvious facial piercing. Wait until you're in a really, really good mood before you undertake any of the above. But not in a really, really good mood because you are totally drunk, please.

OTHER THINGS TO AVOID WHEN DRUNK

* Avoid entering a tattoo parlor.
* Avoid sex with strangers.
* Avoid dialing the phone numbers of ex-boyfriends.
* Avoid dialing the phone numbers of ex-girlfriends.
* Avoid entering into a quick Las Vegas marriage.
* Avoid telling the cute busboy at your regular restaurant how much you've always liked him.
* Avoid placing bets of any kind.
* Avoid joining in a poker game.
* Avoid singing karaoke, unless everyone else is drunker than you.
* No, seriously, your voice doesn't sound as good as you think it does.
* Avoid going into work.
* Avoid drinking even more, because you're "thirsty."
* Avoid calling your boss to tell him how you really felt about what he said to you the day before.
* Avoid signing contracts of any kind.
* Didn't I tell you not to call her?
* Put the phone down.
* Don't text her either.
* Seriously, you will only embarrass yourself.
* Avoid handling caustics, superglue, or hot curling irons.
* Avoid waking up in jail, especially in a strange city.
* Avoid calling your mother, unless you really, really can't get a ride home any other way. Then I'm sure she'll be happy to pick you up, to keep you from driving home drunk.
* Unless she lives out of state.

* Avoid Googling ex-boyfriends or ex-girlfriends, and then e-mailing them.
* If you refuse to listen to me, and start e-mailing everybody, at least make sure your spell-check is on. And keep it short.

SORRY ABOUT THE KHAKIS THING

I mean, if you really love the khakis, and you really look good in them, wear those khakis with pride. Nothing sharper than a white oxford shirt tucked into a pair of khakis. Even not tucked in. It's a classic look. Slip into a pair of scuffed loafers (no socks!) and you and Hemingway are heading over to Harry's Bar to have a scotch. Add a nice worn dark navy cashmere sport coat, and you're off to meet Cary Grant at the Polo Club.

If I sounded less than enthusiastic about the khakis a few sentences back, I was really referring more to the kind of khakis that are so often paired with some bad sweater given at Christmas by great-aunt Tula, who favors those snow-leopard appliqués. Khakis worn without thought are bad khakis. Khakis are boring when they turn into simply pants that you put on in the morning because they're there.

DATING AND YOUR WRITING SKILLS

It doesn't seem possible that spelling and grammar should matter when in pursuit of love, but trust me on this: in this day of e-dating, e-mailing, and instant messaging, there is just something horribly off-putting about seeing "your pretty" in a romantic missive, no matter how sincere the intent. Please, make an attempt to structure your sentences

To paraphrase
Emily Post:

Don't ever write anything
in an e-mail or instant
                 message
that you wouldn't be PROUD to see
Splashed across the
FRONT Page of your Local newspaper.
r u horny
just for instance.

in some kind of grammatically pleasing manner; and if you cannot learn to spell, use your spell-check. The object of your affection will appreciate your going that extra mile. "I would of loved to of seen you last night" just makes me want to unplug the phone and curl up with a good book.

THE BELLS ARE RINGING:
WHAT TO DO FOR THE HAPPY COUPLE

Cousins, brothers, sisters, and the children of old family friends are growing up, too, and a few of them are getting married. You may be invited to some of these weddings, as well as weddings your own friends are having. If your parents are bringing you along as their own action accessory, then you are not necessarily required to bring your own wedding gift, unless you are particularly close friends with the bride or groom. But if you have reached the age where you are getting invited as a single entity apart from your parents, then it would be bad form to not bring a token of some sort.

I am not huge on wedding registries. The faint whiff of acquisitiveness makes me feel vaguely ooky, although I suppose some people find them helpful—perhaps those well-heeled aunties and uncles who are able to purchase complete silver tea services, matching place settings for twenty-four, and whole sets of color-coordinated breakables that may or may not be useful. But if you can barely afford to buy a single silver-plated candlestick, I would advise you to just avoid the whole thing altogether. I'm sure the bride and groom would prefer to be given something simple and useful, as opposed to opening a box and finding one sterling silver fork. I look at the registry as a last resort of suggestions, if I cannot come up with something more personal.

Work on your
Penmanship.
Because, isn't that nice?
And, also, you may want to
write a real letter someday.

If the bride and groom have been cohabitating for a certain amount of time, chances are they already have a good many household appliances and have already bought their own forks. You are not required to purchase toasters and blenders for these people. And if they are just moving in together for the first time after the wedding (which is fairly rare but does happen, especially among the Amish and certain fundamentalist religious sects), you still aren't required to buy them toasters and blenders. Unless you are really good friends and they really need a toaster and you want to get them a toaster, then by all means, go to town. Toasters for everybody!

If you aren't extremely close friends with the bride and groom, you can still put together an interesting grouping of items to make a nice gift. For instance, if they like wine, you could give them a couple of nice bottles, along with two beautiful wine glasses, or a set of little Moroccan tea glasses, which are great for wine and very affordable. A bottle of champagne with two champagne flutes would be a lovely and romantic gift. If they seem to have a sense of humor and/or a love of games, you can give them a set of poker chips, a deck of cards, and a stack of Vegas coasters. Go to a novelty store, and get his 'n' hers whoopee cushions; put them in a basket along with a set of Marx Brothers DVDs and some joy buzzers. A set of schmaltzy, romantic DVD movies along with a big heart-shaped box of chocolates, or a nice picnic basket—the kind that comes with unbreakable wineglasses, plates, and a cheese board—are a fun gift, too. Or go to a little store that carries goods from India, or Korea, or China. You can put together giant baskets of exotic stuff for very little money that anyone would be thrilled to receive as a gift. At least I would. Get creative—there is nothing that says a wedding present has to be stodgy.

If you can't afford anything too extravagant, maybe you can make something yourself, something fun and thoughtful that might have personal meaning to the newlyweds. Make a personalized picture frame; decoupage color-copied photographs of the couple, their dog, or family pictures onto an inexpensive frame from the art supply store, like my friend Peter did once for my birthday.

Restaurant supply shops usually have pretty inexpensive bar supplies; you can purchase a small martini shaker and four martini glasses to put on the really cool tray you're going to make. From the restaurant supply store, get one of those lightweight wooden trays that caterers buy. You can personalize it with a photograph of the couple from their wedding, or their wedding invitation. (Decoupage!) Or you can make it a bar tray, and paint a giant cocktail glass on it. Here's how:

Learn How to Draw a Martini!

(Simply draw a triangle! (see how easy?)

Add an upside-down "T"

Add an oval olive with a small circle inside!

(Add a toothpick)

fig 1: Beginner Martini

mirror the outer shape inside for the liquid

color your inner circle RED like a pimento

OVAL OLIVE

A long oval shape, like a cigar

Make a wide "Y" Shape

(plus the bottom)

ADVANCED OLIVE: OVAL + CIRCLE AT THE TOP WITH A SQUARE INSIDE)

Just play around and have fun!

fig 2: Advanced Martini

Okay, now it's your turn. Even if you're buying a gift, you can get creative, and a gift that obviously had some thought put into it will mean just as much as a set of Lalique finger bowls, if not more.

Your World of Finance!

FIVE-DOLLAR LATTE OR BUY A HOUSE: HOW WILL I EVER DECIDE?

I really have no business giving anyone advice on anything having to do with numbers. Even when well-meaning people talk to me about numbers or attempt to show me any kind of charts or columns involving numbers, my eyes go all wonky and my instinct is to poke my fingers in my ears and sing out, "LA LA LA I CAN'T HEAR YOU."

I grew up in a family that didn't talk about money. Much like a person's religious preference and political leanings, it was just something one didn't discuss in polite company. Yes, it might have been beneficial if my financial education had extended beyond teaching me the correct way to write a check; I suspect my parents assumed that if I had any questions, I would ask. But I didn't know what to ask. I had no financial roadmap. According to my brilliant accountant, Robert, every twentysomething needs a financial "road map" of where they are, and where they want to be.

I know, you are in your twenties, and the idea of forgoing that five-dollar caramel latte today so that you can buy a house, or retire comfortably forty years hence, is laughable. But why not consider this: if you do forgo that overpriced shade-grown Guatemalan, or that grande blended mocha with whipped cream, and opt for your own home brewed (or even the office coffee—hey, it's free!), you could save more than ten thousand dollars over a period of ten years.

Go to Hugh's Mortgage and Financial Calculators Web site (hughchou.org/calc/), where you'll find the "Stop Buying Expensive Coffee and Save" calculator.

You'll also find hughchou.org/calc/coffee.cgi, which figures out exactly how much you will save when you opt for the free office coffee. You'll also find the Booze/Beverage Savings Calculator, and the Gourmet Muffin Calculator. It is a fabulous site that will help you calculate all kinds of things, including a hypothetical mortgage payment, investment returns, how much you would need to invest a month to become a millionaire—and how long it will take you to get there.

According to the financial genius known as my accountant Robert, every young person needs to learn the following financial terms: "plastic surgery" and "frozen assets."

Plastic surgery is the act of taking scissors to one's credit card, and learning to live on cash. An even more creative solution, frozen assets is when you take all your credit cards, place them in a bowl of water, and then place the bowl in the freezer. When the urge strikes to use your credit cards, it will take a mighty effort to unfreeze your assets.

The point is, credit cards aren't an asset, and should not be used as a means to acquire material goods. Yes, it's true, the bank inexplicably gave you a nine-thousand-dollar credit limit, which will buy you a lot of flat-screen TVs and MP3 players. But the cash you earn is an asset, not the fake money represented by your credit cards. If you need to buy a bunch of stuff, buy it with the cash you have, or you will be very, very sorry when you realize at the end of the month that you only have enough money to pay the minimum payment on your credit card. If you continue to pay off only the minimum payment on a credit card bill, it could take you the rest of your life, and you might still only be paying off the interest on that card. You will be chipping away at your debt, while the interest piles up, and grows larger and larger.

When you use credit cards to buy stuff you think you need, you are borrowing money. It is not free to borrow money. If you don't allow yourself to use credit cards to buy stuff you need, you will think long and hard about whether you really need to buy that stuff. We live in a credit-happy country, where irresponsible behavior is empowered by credit cards and rewarded with offers of even more credit cards. And who exactly is being enriched by this system? Hint: not you.

If you choose to use a credit card, because using it will garner you airline flights or rewards of some sort, then you are getting your money to work for you, but only if you pay it off in full at the end of each month.

Eating out three or four times a week can add up, even if it's "cheap" takeout. And if you're putting those occasional meals on an already existing credit card balance, you are now paying interest on the fried rice you had a month ago. Ouch. That is some pricey fried rice.

My personal financial wizard Robert also tells young people that the best way to double your money is to fold it in half and put in your wallet. I bet the kids love that. But it's very good advice; don't spend your money buying a lot of crap that you don't need. Keep it in your pants, so to speak. Or in the bank, at a good interest rate. A CD (certificate of deposit) usually has a higher return than a savings account; for the best return of all, invest in either real estate or the stock market. Both have their ups and downs, but both always move higher.

Super CPA Robert also asks this question: "Would you rather receive a million dollars today or the result of a penny doubled every day for thirty days?" Most people jump on the million dollars, but if you double that little penny every day for thirty more days, on the thirty-first day it becomes worth ten million seven hundred thirty-seven thousand four hundred eighteen dollars.

Really! Look:

Day 1
$0.01 Your penny, worth, well, one cent.

Day 2
$0.02 It's only two cents.

Day 3
$0.04 Yup, four cents. You've doubled your money.

Day 4
$0.08 It's already day four, and I've got eight cents.

Day 5
$0.16 Right. Sixteen cents is going to get me ten million dollars. Right.

Day 6
$0.32 Thirty-two cents. Oh, why, why didn't I take the million when it was offered?

Day 7
$0.64 Tell me it's not too late to take the million.

Day 8

$1.28 A dollar twenty-eight won't even
get me a blended mocha.

Day 9

$2.56 Great.

Day 10

$5.12 Five bucks and twelve cents.
I don't see where this is going.

Day 11

$10.24 Just call me lucky.

Day 12

$20.48 I cannot retire on twenty bucks.

Day 13

$40.96 Only forty bucks, and it's already day
thirteen.

Day 14

$81.92 This is not looking good.

Day 15

$163.84 Yeah, yeah.

Day 16
$327.68 This will go far.

Day 17
$655.36 This won't even pay my rent.

Day 18
$1,310.72 Okay, I'm just going to go into the other room and whimper quietly.

Day 19
$2,621.44

Day 20
$5,242.88

Day 21
$10,485.76

Day 22
$20,971.52

Day 23
$41,943.04

Day 24
$83,886.08

Day 25
$167,772.16

Day 26
$335,544.32 Okay, not like this is bad. It's good.
But we're still not that close to a million.

Day 27
$671,088.64 Okay, we're closer.

Day 28
$1,342,177.28 Now that is an amazing
one-day return.

Day 29
$2,684,354.56 I am so glad I didn't take the million.

Day 30
$5,368,709.12 Patience really does have its rewards.

Day 31
$10,737,418.24 You took the million? Suckah.

Now, obviously there are no investments that will double our money on a daily basis, but it still illustrates how quickly a small investment will grow, and how saving a little money, bit by bit, over time, in a steady, tortoiselike manner, will win you the race.

If you want to save for that starter home, but your idea of a starter home is a million-dollar spread in a top neighborhood, it may take you a while. But if you can lower your sights to a realistic level and start closer to the bottom, you can eventually work your way up to your dream house. HUD foreclosures, VA foreclosures, and other government programs along with bank foreclosures (referred to as REOs, or real estate owned) can be better alternatives for first timers than hiring a realtor and paying full freight on a fixer-upper. And when you do finally get to buy your first house, you will need excellent credit, especially if you want to get a good rate. You will even need good credit for renting an apartment, so use your credit card to build that perfect credit, by paying off your balance in full and on time every month.

You don't necessarily have to live like a monk in order to save money for your future. After all, life is for living, and no one wants to be the bitter, penny-pinching miser who lies on his deathbed with a million simolians under his mattress but no friends to visit him.

We all need to feel rewarded for our hard work. Socializing, throwing parties, cooking a nice meal for friends, giving gifts, having a comfortable place to call home, occasionally wearing some natty threads or buying a fancy coffee are just some of the ways in which we like to reward ourselves from time to time. But your rewards don't have to be expensive ones, nor should you be paying for those little rewards with interest for the next forty years. Happy memories can be had without breaking the bank.

I know you are a fabulous person who thinks he deserves to drive a sporty and expensively named automobile. I know you're special, and you shouldn't have to *take the bus* with a lot of losers who are too loser-y to own their own cars. And so what if it costs two hundred dollars to fill the gas tank of your obscenely large, canary-yellow, modified army desert vehicle that gets under ten miles to the gallon? You're worth it!

And it's only fair that you should get to carry that handbag with somebody else's giant initials emblazoned on the front, containing a tiny, overbred dog. Of course your purse is totally worth the three thousand dollars you spent on it. Those corporate initials can really cost a lot!

But think of how rewarded you might feel if, by scrimping, saving, and making a few sacrifices, you woke up ten years from now to discover you had saved enough to buy a house, or to travel around the world, or to buy a plot of land, and that your retirement fund had exponentially grown to such a degree that you could contemplate actually retiring before the age of fifty. Wouldn't that feel better than getting dirty looks because your gas-guzzling monstrosity is single-handedly causing a rapid acceleration of global warming? Isn't saving for something substantial perhaps worth more than impressing dates, neighbors, and the valet parking guy?

Rearrange your priorities. If you are living paycheck to paycheck, most of your paycheck should not be going toward making a monthly payment on a luxury car and eating out at restaurants.

Credit Card Tip: If you do have a credit card, I hope you are paying it off in full every month, but it still can't hurt to try to bring your rate down as low as possible. First, call up a few different credit card companies and express interest in acquiring a new credit card. While they are salivating, ask them what kind of low rate they can give you. Then call your credit card company and ask if they can go any lower on your rate, saying you are thinking of switching to another card that has a lower rate. Presumably your credit card company wants your business, and if they are smart they will immediately fall all over themselves to give you a lower rate. They will jack the rate back up if you are late on a payment, so be good and pay on time.

HOW TO GO A WHOLE DAY WITHOUT SPENDING MONEY

Let's just say that when you get a wad of cash, you cannot spend it fast enough. It starts burning a hole in your pocket, and nothing short of a brand new pair of shoes, fuzzy dice, or a blowout at the local club will scratch that itch.

First of all, make sure you've got food in the house. Then challenge yourself to go a whole day, if not a whole week, without spending any money. You can do it! And it will feel really good afterward, when you make a rough tally of how much money you saved..

Invite friends over instead of going out to a bar after work. Have a potluck. Mmm, casseroles! Pack your own lunch every day for a month. But what else can you do?

* Go to the library and check out a stack of books.
* Go to the library and check out some DVDs.

✳ Do you even have a library card? Get one! There's a bunch of free stuff in there you can borrow!

✳ Drink water with ice and lemon instead of those horrible diet sodas to which you've become addicted. Honestly, the aftertaste? Woof!

✳ Instead of shopping for clothes, go to a newsstand and peruse the fashion magazines.

✳ Instead of shopping for clothes, go through your closet and be amazed at how much stuff you already have.

✳ Take this opportunity to organize what you already do have, culling all the clothes you haven't worn for two years or more. Give to friends or a charity that will do something useful with them.

✳ Read one of those books you checked out of the library.

✳ Call your local museum and find out when they offer free admission days or evenings. Then invite some friends for an outing to the museum.

✳ Call your local museum and find out if they offer free movie screenings.

✳ Pick up a local free weekly paper and check listings for free events.

✳ Take a walk to a friend's house instead of driving.

✳ Look for loose change in your sofa.

✳ Oh, and did I mention? Make sure you have food in the house.

✳ Instead of shopping, go to a good friend's house with an armload of clothes you no longer wear, and trade them in for any garments your friend wants to unload. Look, you're recycling!

HEY, MR. ARTSY PANTS

If you decide to be a self-employed or freelance writer, actor, or artist of any kind: Good luck! It is really much, much harder than it looks, and I advise you to love what you do so much that you'll be able to stomach the constant roller-coaster ride that will be your life. You will have very little financial stability, consistency, or security. You must weather feast and famine, and attempt to budget each month even though you may not have a steady paycheck. You will need to resist the urge to spend like a sailor when you finally do get those long-awaited financial rewards for your artistic endeavors. You will have to have the patience of a saint, learn to live like a monk, and be as crazy as a bedbug. Okay, not so much the last bit, but hackneyed similes are really addictive, aren't they?

In any event, it's not an easy life. But you're a creative person, so get creative! Learn to be resourceful. Live creatively.

You won't be watching much TV, because you'll be too busy painting, or writing that novel, or looking for seedy clubs in which you can play your jazz clarinet; so you may not need the extra monthly expense of cable. You may not need a TV at all. Your dwelling need not be a doorman apartment, or even a fancy "artist's loft" in the middle of the recently gentrified and overpriced warehouse—s'cuse me, "arts" district. You need a place to work and a place to sleep. Perhaps a converted garage, or a room above someone's garage, or someone's guesthouse, or a one-room apartment above a dim sum restaurant. It will only add to your cachet as an artist to live, for a time, in a crappy studio in a colorfully seamy (but preferably not too dangerous) part of town.

If you can manage this in one of our well-planned metropolitan areas, you won't need a car at all, which will save you a lot of money.

New York, Chicago, Seattle, Portland, and San Francisco are just a few cities that have practical and mostly efficient public transportation systems. And the traffic is usually so bad, and parking so difficult to find, that keeping a car in these cities is only expensive and pointless. The thousands of dollars you won't be paying for fuel, parking, and insurance will help you buy paint or paper, or whatever tools you might need to aid in your creative process. A used bicycle will help you get around locally, when you want to zip over to the art supply store or over to your local theatre for rehearsals. And cities with good transportation systems are also usually good walking cities, too.

If you don't get a regular paycheck, it might be helpful to be able to, say, pay half your rent on the first of the month and half in the middle of the month. It can't hurt to ask your landlord if he might be amenable to this arrangement. He might also be open to the idea of your doing a little gardening, or painting, or fix-it stuff, for a little break in your rent. You'll never know if you don't ask.

Since you have some kind of talent, or are at least under the impression that you do, you have the means to barter, which is a wonderful way to save a pile of dough. Perhaps the dim sum restaurant downstairs will take your services in trade for a certain number of lunches or dinners—you could paint a mural on their wall, or design a new menu for the restaurant, or paint a sign for their sidewalk. I once traded a drawing for a case of spaghetti sauce (thanks, Mr. DelGrosso!) and did a painting in exchange for some handyman work. You may not be able to parlay your talents into meals, goods, and services with Mr. Giant Corporation, but you may possibly have some luck bartering with your friendly local tradesperson. Do you have a talent that might be valuable to someone else?

Living the freelance life doesn't necessarily mean living from hand to mouth, but it can. So save money when you can, and learn to live as frugally as possible.

There are many wonderful things about living on the slightly un-predictable outer edge of the conventional workforce, which I'm sure you've figured out by now. Yes, we can stay in our pajamas all day if we want, and our time is completely our own to budget. But budget it you must, or you'll be in very sad pajamas, bumming rent money and living on carrots and cat food. If you do manage to budget, you will be re-warded with vacations at odd times, no clock to punch in the morning, and better coffee than you'll usually find in an office kitchen.

BUDGETING YOUR LIFE: BORING, BUT SO SATISFYING!

Try making a budget for yourself as a way to see how much you really have to live on, as opposed to how much you wish you had. Wishful thinking leads to excessive credit card use, and that ultimately leads to you, at the age of forty-five, paying off the interest on a skirt you bought when you were twenty-five.

Identify your expenses as fixed or variable. Fixed expenses are those that occur each month and are usually for the same amount. Examples of fixed expenses are your rent, car payment, and, although I hope you don't have any, your consumer debt payments. Fixed expenses are un-likely to change. You can control variable expenses such as utility bills (by conserving energy and cutting back on long-distance phone calls), groceries (do you really need that filet mignon?), and entertainment (go to a low-priced matinee and don't buy popcorn).

Thinking about your expenses in this way will help you identify the expenses you *can* change if you want to or need to.

Remember that not all your expenses—fixed or variable—will occur every month. For example, if you have a car, then you must buy insur-ance; car insurance premiums are often paid only twice a year, and can be a nasty surprise if you haven't set the money aside ahead of time. But if you take the annual amount and divide it by twelve months, you can account for the expense in your budget as a "savings" item each month so you will be prepared to pay the bill when it arrives.

Here are a few ways to help you figure out your yearly expenses:

If you decide to live on your own, or with roommates other than your parents: Estimate the cost of housing in the area where you plan to live by calling various rental properties or looking at local listings. Add up the prices, and compute an average. You should expect to spend from 25 to 30 percent of your monthly net income on housing.

Utilities: You will also need to budget for utilities, such as gas and electricity, if they are not already included in your rent. Try to get them included in your rent, especially if you decide to live in an incredibly cold climate. Do not forget the costs of a telephone. If you will not be living near your family, long-distance telephone calls may be a significant budget item. E-mailing is a wonderful thing. Budget from 2 to 10 percent of your net income for utilities.

Transportation: In general, you can expect to spend from 2 to 5 percent of your net income on transportation. Obviously, public transportation is much less expensive than owning a car.

Food and Personal: Personal items and food costs include clothing, groceries, entertainment, dining out, cleaning, and haircuts. If you keep a day-by-day record of your expenses for a month or so, you will have a good idea how much you spend on these items. You can estimate that you will spend from 10 to 15 percent of your net income for food and from 2 to 10 percent for personal expenses.

Debt Obligations and Insurance: To avoid excessive debt expense, you should try to spend no more than 5 to 15 percent of your net income for monthly payments on student loans and consumer debts, including credit cards and car payments. Your health insurance, auto, and renter's/home owner's insurance payments are usually fixed amounts, but they might not be paid on a monthly basis. You should budget from 2 to 5 percent of your monthly net income for these expenses.

Savings: I know it isn't easy, but try to put from 5 to 10 percent of your net earnings into a savings account. I only wish I had known this when I was your age. This money can be set aside for unexpected expenses, emergencies, or vacations. Your employer may offer a pretax savings plan, often called a 401(k) account, a 403(b) account, or "annuity." This type of plan allows you to save for your future and reduces the amount of income tax you pay. If you are self-employed and sit home writing books and scrounging for work, you will not have the benefit of a 401(k), and in fact may have only a vague idea of what a 401(k) might be, in which case you should just attempt to put ten or twenty bucks into your savings account on a weekly basis, or whenever you possibly can.

Miscellaneous: Because you cannot predict every monthly expense, you should set aside from 1 to 2 percent of your monthly net income for miscellaneous expenses. These could include convenience items, magazines, newspapers, and other small purchases.

Savings Tip: Subscribing to magazines is a better value than buying them off the newsstands, especially if you know you are going to want to read every issue of a certain magazine or two. Why not share a subscription with a friend? Or, if you have a friend who already has a few magazine subscriptions, ask your friend if you can have the magazines after they've been read. (Unless your friends like to keep back issues. Then find someone else to mooch off.)

* The best way to save money on a car is to buy a late-model used car and drive it until it's junk. For a little more money, you can

get a very well cared for, used (preowned!) automobile if you
purchase a lease return. A car loses 30 percent of its value in
the first year.

✳ Resist the urge to buy the latest computer, MP3 player, or other
gadget the minute it comes out. Take a deep breath and wait at
least three months; the price will go down.

✳ Wait for the second generation of any new computer model;
they will have worked out some of the peskier kinks.

✳ Buy airline tickets as early as you possibly can. Most seats go on
sale eleven months in advance, and the cheapest fares are the
first to go.

Kiplinger.com has a wealth (ha!) of free financial advice, and I would
encourage, no, insist you read anything Suze Orman, especially *The
Money Book for the Young, Fabulous & Broke.* She is the diva of dollars
and will teach you everything you will ever need to know to pull yourself out of whatever financial mess you're in.

IT'S APRIL 15: DO YOU KNOW WHERE YOUR TAXES ARE?

I have been avoiding writing the section about taxes like most people
avoid doing their actual taxes. But okay, take a deep breath and sit
down, possibly with a comforting beverage. Taxes are an inevitable part
of life—and a necessary one, if you want to live in a civilized society.
Our taxes help pay for filling up those potholes in the streets, keeping the freeways from collapsing, and educating our children. Wait a
minute, you say; I don't have any kids! Why should I pay to educate
other people's children? Well, because if you don't help support public
education through your taxes, roving bands of illiterate and angry youth

will roam the streets and steal your wallet, or something like that. It's one of those things that is Good for Society. Sometimes I have to pay for stupid wars I don't believe in, and sometimes people whose parents sent them to private schools don't understand why they need to pony up for public school kids. You just do, because it's the right thing to do to support the community. Plus, you'll get in really, really big trouble if you don't.

If you work, you have to pay taxes, state and federal. If taxes are taken out of your paycheck, and even if you know you won't owe any, you still have to fill out the tax forms and send them in by April 15. You may get a refund, depending upon how much was taken out of your paycheck compared with how much you owe the IRS. Doing taxes is not the most unpleasant task in the world, but it certainly goes easier if you have saved your relevant receipts in an envelope or accordion file, or a shoe box, and have kept good track of what you can and cannot write off.

Start early, preferably in December or January. Do not wait until April 12, or you will be frantic and unhappy, and most surely need to file an extension. Filing an extension is not the end of the world, but it's so much nicer to be done with it all before the deadline, and the earlier the better.

Before you even sit down with tax documents and receipts, you'll need to make certain that you have all the necessary forms and schedules. You can request the forms and schedules you need from the Internal Revenue Service (IRS) by phone or online.

You may want to consider using tax-preparation software to prepare your taxes on your home computer. If you use tax software, you won't have to worry about securing the proper forms, as tax forms and schedules are apparently included with the software. You can even download updated forms over the Internet and import them into the program. Or, you can also go directly to the IRS Web site and use the "e-file" feature to file and pay your taxes. Not that I've ever done that, but I've heard it's a breeze.

Make sure that you have all the tax documents that you'll need. They can be easy to misplace, so as they show up in the mail, put them in a safe place. Gather your 1099s, W-2s, dividend statements, and other tax-related documents and check them for errors. Do this early. Do everything related to your taxes early, in case you have to wait for corrected documents.

If you did taxes last year, it would be a good idea to have last year's tax return handy as you prepare to do your taxes. Look at last year's deductions and information, and you'll get a good idea of what to do this year. Also, ask your parents if there are any stocks or investments in your name that you might not know about.

Once you are sure that your tax documents are in order, you might want to get a calculator, a few sharpened pencils, and some scratch paper. If you're using software to prepare your taxes, you may not need to perform as many calculations. However, it's a good idea to keep such supplies handy for double-checking figures and adding receipts together without using your fingers.

The last thing you should do before you start doing your taxes is to go to the IRS Web site for any changes or news relating to the tax laws. And if you are still confused, take advantage of people more knowledgeable than you; ask questions of parents and informed friends. If you're really stumped, offer to take a friend who's a tax expert out for coffee, so you can ask questions and take some notes.

If you have a little extra scratch this year, are working freelance and self-employed (one year I had forty-three W-4s), or if you just start breaking into a cold sweat/hives at the thought of doing your taxes, spring for a tax preparer. A good tax preparer or accountant will take care of everything for you, for a fee. It is often worth the price, especially if they find that you have a little refund that you didn't know you had coming. They will usually need all of your bank statements for the year, and all of your business-related receipts; it's a good idea to have kept track of your mileage for the year, if you think you are entitled to write it off.

IF YOU HAVE LOTS AND LOTS OF MONEY

Let's say you are in that small, elite minority of the favored few; you are rich, rich, rich! Well, then, you really need to know how to behave, because whether you have new money or old, a great number of your lot are behaving in an increasingly arrogant and obnoxious manner. Most people in the world are not as monetarily well endowed as you, so it's important to be sensitive to that fact when you are around them.

You will also find that some of the most interesting people in society are not from the top rungs of the social and economic ladder, and if you want to hang out with interesting people, you'll need to know how to behave, so you can adapt to any kind of social gathering.

Also, your father or mother having earned or inherited an inordinate amount of money does not make you a superior person. I'm sorry, but it doesn't, and you know that, deep down inside. You may have a lot of money. You may have always had a lot of money. But it is your parents' money, and you didn't earn it yourself.

And if you did earn all that money, if you currently have an incredibly high-paying job that makes you more than your entire high school graduating class, you still don't get to act like a jerk. Again, I'm sorry. I know you might have been under the impression that once you became a member of the moneyed classes you got to automatically behave like an asshole, but it's not really true. Many rich people are under this misapprehension.

That's right; just because you have a lot of money, whether it's your hard-earned cash or your grandfather's, you still need to know how to treat people nicely and with respect. And although I cannot believe you are not totally embarrassed driving around town in that outsized, faux-military, luxury vehicle that is more suited to a mountainous terrain than a crowded street, you are not allowed to run stop signs and cut people off. And do you really need such a big, stupid car?

I know, it's your money, and you can do what you like with it; but as in everything in life, it's always good to put some thought behind the way you live your life. You may just really feel the need to buy a ridiculously overpriced and conspicuous car, just because you can. But you will be inheriting this world, and its resources are not unlimited, nor are they just for you alone to use.

Also, when you are out at a really expensive restaurant, your waiter or waitress is not actually your own personal slave. That is not his job. His job is to tell you what the chef's specials are, and to serve you food, in a prompt and hopefully cheerful manner. Treating your waitperson like an indentured servant will do nothing for your allure; lording it over the busboy does not bring out your most shining qualities. Ordering people about actually makes you look more like an arrogant ass, and less like an elegant person of means. And it is such a cliché! I mean honestly, you don't want to be a walking cliché, do you? Don't give a bad name to the wealthy. It's already difficult enough for rich people, what with all the household help they need, and the expensive handbags, and the greed and the plaid, and being a Republican and having to defend those ridiculous tax breaks and all.

Think before you start accessorizing your life with the really unnecessary. Do you know that you will have to give that tiny dog water every three hours or it will die of dehydration? Did you know that an eight-thousand-dollar handbag could buy updated textbooks for several public high school science classes? Anybody with money can buy an expensive designer handbag, but how many really imaginative individuals will go over to the local public elementary school and donate eight thousand dollars' worth of art supplies? Just a thought, next time all that cash is just burning a hole in your Gucci gauchos. There are plenty of wealthy people who don't dress, or drive, or travel or live as if they are rolling in dough, which means they will always have plenty to be comfortable, and probably have a little extra to spread around in their community.

Just because you carry a platinum credit card, you still need to say please and thank you, and hold doors open for elderly people carrying packages. You still need to know how to look people in the eyes and say hello.

And try not to judge people on the make of their car or the label on their jeans—or lack of label. Avoid saying utterly clueless things like, "How can anyone live on less than a hundred thousand dollars a year?"—even if you really think it. The person you said it to might live on considerably less. Don't make assumptions about people based on how much money you think they have. Because that would be the opposite of what a well-bred person would do, in case you were trying to give an impression of one.

SERIOUS SELF-SUFFICIENCY: NO
BLOW DRYER? WE'RE ALL GONNA DIE!

Imagine if suddenly there were no electricity, no fuel for transportation, no manicures or happy hours—would you be one of those people who would just collapse under the strain of it? Would you fall apart at the idea of having to wear sensible shoes and forage for food? You may live in an urban or suburban environment, with every amenity and modern convenience at your fingertips; you may live there for the very reason that you have no desire to grow your own food or harness energy from your downspout, or raise chickens.

I have friends who might prefer death if living meant not wearing five-inch heels and hailing a cab to their favorite bistro. What kind of a life does not include blasting the air conditioner in their SUV or keeping a lawn green in a desert climate? Not a life they want to live. Of course we can only hope that we'll have unlimited reality shows and daily news updates on the weight fluctuations of celebrities for years to come, but one way to help ensure a life filled with the kind of abundance to which we are all too accustomed is to conserve everything you can, when you possibly can. Self-sufficiency isn't just about knowing how to boil an egg and pay your taxes, it's about being self-sufficient on a global level, too.

If you aren't already recycling your cans, bottles, and other recyclables, um, why aren't you, again? Is it just "too much trouble" to put your cans and bottles and recyclables into a recycle bin? I might be somewhat understanding if you had to lug bags of cans and bottles and piles of newspapers and magazines on a ten-mile bus ride to the recycling center, but most cities and towns in these modern times employ big, shiny green recycling trucks, who will come to your house or apartment and pick up your bin full of recyclables. There are hardly any excuses left to not recycle. It's about the easiest thing you can do, since burly guys wearing gloves are usually the ones who have to actually sort through everything, not you.

So, recycle your garbage. And bring a reusable shopping bag with you next time you are getting a small load of groceries, too.

Change all your regular or incandescent light bulbs over to compact fluorescent light bulbs. Changing one light bulb doesn't seem like much, but compact fluorescent bulbs use 60 percent less energy than regular light bulbs, and will save about three hundred pounds of carbon dioxide per year, which might help stave off some of the consequences of global warming. Buy recycled paper products, which take from 70 to 90 percent less energy to produce *and* might help save our forests.

Replacing a dirty air filter on your furnace can save hundreds of pounds of carbon dioxide a year. Use warm or cold water, instead of hot, to do your laundry (five hundred pounds a year saved), and if you are buying appliances, choose energy efficient models. Plant a tree! Ride a bike! Buy locally grown produce and food! More tips can be found at climatecrisis.org, where you will also find a handy calculator that will help you calculate your environmental footprint.

Just try not to take up so much space, is all I'm saying. We all have to share our resources, and you will get a warm, cozy, satisfied feeling deep down inside, knowing that you are doing as much as you can to make your footprint on this planet just a little smaller. Yes, your friends may chuckle at the compost pail full of food scraps next to your kitchen sink. They may make snide remarks when you ask to take the coffee grounds home from their dinner party for your compost pile. They may even think your worm bin is "disgusting" and "weird," but come tomato season, who's dropping by unexpectedly and hinting around for home-grown vegetables?

The actual garbage that you will end up throwing into the garbage can will be whittled down to at least half, and you'll save gallons of water not disposing of stuff down the disposal. All that, and you'll end up with piles of rich, nutritious compost or worm castings for your garden or houseplants. Or sell it to your friends; who's laughing now?

Your local Parks and Recreation or gardening center might have more information, or go to the Internet and find a site much like composters. com to look at a profusion of comely composting containers for indoor and outdoor use. I am not kidding about the worm bins, people. You can keep them indoors, you really can. And those busy babies will not only dispose of banana peels, apple cores, fruit and vegetable peels, pits and leaves, but also coffee grounds, tea leaves, paper towels, paper napkins, and in fact, everything short of bones and hunks of cheese. And two thousand red wigglers in a container under your kitchen counter are sure to be a conversation starter!

DON'T LEAVE THE WATER RUNNING WHILE YOU BRUSH YOUR TEETH!

1. Wet your toothbrush. Turn off the water.
2. Apply toothpaste to your toothbrush.
3. Brush your teeth. Spit.
4. Rinse your mouth and your brush briefly, with water.
5. Turn the water off, and inadvertently save hundreds of gallons of water.

There, that wasn't so hard, was it?

If Your Mom Still
Chews Your Food for You

WHOA, DUDE! AREN'T YOUR ROOMMATES, LIKE, KIND OF OLD?

You really are thinking about it, aren't you? You're thinking about moving back in with Mom and Dad. I mean, after all, rent is enormously expensive, and you both live in the same town, right?

Oh, I guess if you all really get along well, and you pay your parents a fair rent, and you pitch in with the dishwashing and cooking and leaf raking and grocery buying, and you get your own phone line, and possibly your own entrance, well, it might work out. And certainly if your parents need a little extra help, or are having health problems, or they really want you to move back so you can give them a hand with your wheelchair-bound grandma, then you would be doing a good thing for your family, and you are probably a wonderful person who can just skip to the next chapter. But if you want to move back in because it's cheaper and you want your mom to do your laundry and cook your meals, well, you need to disabuse yourself of that notion immediately.

Yes, it's hard being on your own; it's not easy paying your own rent and making your own meals. And if you expect to have a fabulous downtown loft with a view of the city lights, then yes, you will need a pretty high-paying job to get yourself something like that, and it may not happen right away. You might need to set your sights a little lower, find less expensive living quarters, and share the rent with a few roommates. You might need some time to climb the ladder.

Now, if your parents are very rich and generous, and are helping you out for a little while after college so that you can get on your feet, then you are very fortunate. But don't allow them to subsidize your lifestyle just because you think you deserve to live in a three-thousand-square-foot apartment and drive a luxury vehicle. If they are helping you out so you can save money for further education or travel, then that is very nice of them. But you will need to learn to be on your own sooner or later, you will need to know how to budget and pay your own way, and living with Mom and Dad will only postpone the inevitable.

Plus, I mean, stop taking money from Mom and Dad. Are you twelve?

YOUR VERY CARING PARENTS: CUTTING YOURSELF OFF LIFE SUPPORT

Why do you leave your crumbs all over the counter after you toast your bagel? Do you imagine that your invisible mommy will be cleaning up after you? Not to say that this is entirely your fault. Apparently Mommy and Daddy loved you so much they thought they would make your life easier by doing everything for you.

For instance, I am almost certain that you didn't build that to-scale model of the White House when you were in second grade. The mortise-and-tenon construction was kind of a tip-off, as were the tiny electrical lights. Yes, Mommy really wanted you to get a good grade on that seventh grade essay, which is why she pretty much wrote it herself, but she wasn't doing you any favors. Daddy may have thought he was helping you when he yelled at your Little League coach for calling you out, but he was really just making your transition to adulthood that much more difficult.

Well, it's time to clue Mom and Dad in. It's time to tell Mom to stop chewing your food for you, and Dad to stop filling your gas tank. As much as they want to smooth your bumpy road, cushion all the sharp corners, and make life easier for you, you need to start learning how to navigate life by yourself. It's a wonderful thing to have a close relationship with your parents, and to be able to go to them for advice, or an occasional hot meal. It's one thing if you have a close-knit family and you all like to hang out together from time to time. But if you are visiting your mother so that she can do your laundry, or worse, inviting her over to your place so she can clean your bathroom, it is time to change the nature of your relationship.

Your mother may think she is just giving you a hand, but she is not your maid. She is your mother. You are allowed to accept the occasional pot of chicken soup, or other homemade specialty. And if she is a talented seamstress and really wants to sew you some curtains, that is very generous of her.

If your father knows a lot about car engines, or filling out a tax form, and you need some guidance in that area, well of course you can ask him for help. He'll probably be happy to give it, just as any friend would. But he should not be bailing you out of jail or paying your gambling debts. He should not pay off your overdrawn credit card unless you plan on paying him back, with interest, on a monthly basis. If your mom and dad magically make your mistakes disappear, it will seem as if those bad things never happened, and then those bad things might just happen again.

And why shouldn't they? If you've never squirmed under the burden of shame or embarrassment, if you've never had to feel the pain of humiliation because of the consequences of your moronic actions, then it's probable that you will continue to make unfortunate decisions in the future. Your parents need to stop childproofing your life, and you need to help them. It's time for you to venture out and start up the road to adulthood. Just say "no" to coddling.

Part of being an adult is doing things for other people. Maybe you could offer to help out your mom and dad for a change. Make them a loaf of banana bread, or a nice dinner. Or take them out to a good restaurant, if you're feeling a little flush. Assert your autonomy by demonstrating how self-sufficient you really are.

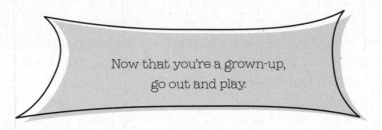

Now that you're a grown-up,
go out and play.

VOTE

Vote, vote, vote.
Make voting part of your life.
Have election night parties.
Wear that little stickum flag proudly.
Encourage your friends and neighbors to vote.
Vote in every single election.

Go to: factcheck.org
Nonpartisan research into the latest
headlines and campaign advertisements.

BUY, BORROW, OR SUBSCRIBE TO THESE MAGAZINES

Ready-Made: The most fun and informative how-to magazine on the newsstand. Get it for the "Martha Lives!" and the clever "MacGyver" sections, which challenge readers to come up with clever uses for dead pens, old jeans, and other assorted cast-offs.

Saveur: A food lover's nirvana. Lush photographs you could just eat with a spoon, interesting food trivia, great recipes for authentic world cuisine, along with a yearly "Top 100" issue that is sublime!

Dwell: Forward-looking design, inspiring modern prefab architecture, and ideas for small-space dwelling.

Bust: For Women with Something to Get off Their Chests. Their words, not mine. It's smart, sassy, humorous, and full o' information for the gals. Boys'll like it, too.

In the summer, place a dryer sheet in your pocket. It will keep the mosquitoes away. Or so I've heard.

DO YOU KNOW?

All right, let's assume you're groomed, and dressed, and have made your bed. But will I be able to have a conversation with you? Are the few bits of knowledge that you have retained from your years of education just bouncing around aimlessly with little company? Yes, cooking and cleaning skills are valuable to have, and nice manners are important, but you also want to be able to break the ice at a party, or talk to your girlfriend or boyfriend when you've finished doing other things.

Do you know . . . ?

* Anything about opera?
* How many men and women serve on the Supreme Court?
* The names of your state representatives in Congress?
* How to dance a waltz?
* Anything about Coleman Hawkins?
* Any constellations? Any at all? Oh for God's sake, they're out there every night! Learn a few!
* The names of your senators?
* What Mary Pickford, Charlie Chaplin, and Douglas Fairbanks did?
* Anything about Lenny Bruce?
* The names of the Marx Brothers?
* Which Beatle played bass?
* What team Mickey Mantle played for?
* The names of the seven deadly sins?
* What was in the Zapruder film?
* Van Gogh: Which ear? (Just kidding.)

It wouldn't be a bad idea to get E. D. Hirsch Jr.'s *New Dictionary of Cultural Literacy,* if you don't already have it. A very handy book to have around. Also, *Lies My Teacher Told Me* by James W. Loewen. Everything your American history textbook got wrong!

Special Game Show Box by Special Guest Writer Richard Goldman

One of the biggest problems on Capitol Hill is pork barrel legislation. With that in mind, can you tell which of the following is the name of a current or former U.S. senator, and which is a breed of pig? Answer "senator" or "swine." Play with your friends!

(Answers at the bottom of the page. If you can read tiny writing without reading glasses, cover up the answers before playing.)

1. Dutch Landrace
2. Saxby Chambliss
3. Sam Brownback
4. Wessex Saddleback
5. Red Wattle
6. Orrin Hatch
7. Mora Romagnola
8. Olympia Snowe
9. Swabian Hall
10. Chester White
11. Lincoln Chafee

(1. Swine 2. R-Georgia 3. R-Kansas 4. Swine 5. Swine 6. R-Utah 7.Swine 8. R-Maine 9. Swine 10. Swine 11. R-Rhode Island)

DO YOU KNOW . . . WHAT'S IN THE BILL OF RIGHTS?

Amendments 1–10 of the Constitution

The Conventions of a number of the States having, at the time of adopting the Constitution, expressed a desire, in order to prevent misconstruction or abuse of its powers, that further declaratory and restrictive clauses should be added, and as extending the ground of public confidence in the Government will best insure the beneficent ends of its institution;

Resolved, by the Senate and House of Representatives of the United States of America, in Congress assembled, two-thirds of both Houses concurring, that the following articles be proposed to the Legislatures of the several States, as amendments to the Constitution of the United States; all or any of which articles, when ratified by three-fourths of the said Legislatures, to be valid to all intents and purposes as part of the said Constitution, namely:

Amendment I
Congress shall make no law respecting an establishment of religion, or prohibiting the free exercise thereof; or abridging the freedom of speech, or of the press; or the right of the people peaceably to assemble, and to petition the government for a redress of grievances.

Amendment II
A well-regulated militia, being necessary to the security of a free State, the right of the people to keep and bear arms, shall not be infringed.

Amendment III

No soldier shall, in time of peace be quartered in any house, without the consent of the owner, nor in time of war, but in a manner to be prescribed by law.

Amendment IV

The right of the people to be secure in their persons, houses, papers, and effects, against unreasonable searches and seizures, shall not be violated, and no warrants shall issue, but upon probable cause, supported by oath or affirmation, and particularly describing the place to be searched, and the persons or things to be seized.

Amendment V

No person shall be held to answer for a capital, or otherwise infamous crime, unless on a presentment or indictment of a grand jury, except in cases arising in the land or naval forces, or in the militia, when in actual service in time of war or public danger; nor shall any person be subject for the same offense to be twice put in jeopardy of life or limb; nor shall be compelled in any criminal case to be a witness against himself, nor be deprived of life, liberty, or property, without due process of law; nor shall private property be taken for public use, without just compensation.

Amendment VI

In all criminal prosecutions, the accused shall enjoy the right to a speedy and public trial, by an impartial jury of the State and district wherein the crime shall have been committed, which district shall have been previously ascertained by law, and to be informed of the nature and cause of the accusation; to be confronted with the witnesses against him; to have compulsory process for obtaining witnesses in his favor, and to have the assistance of counsel for his defense.

Amendment VII
In suits at common law, where the value in controversy shall exceed twenty dollars, the right of trial by jury shall be preserved, and no fact tried by a jury, shall be otherwise reexamined in any court of the United States, than according to the rules of the common law.

Amendment VIII
Excessive bail shall not be required, nor excessive fines imposed, nor cruel and unusual punishments inflicted.

Amendment IX
The enumeration in the Constitution, of certain rights, shall not be construed to deny or disparage others retained by the people.

Amendment X
The powers not delegated to the United States by the Constitution, nor prohibited by it to the States, are reserved to the States respectively, or to the people.

IF ONLY I HAD KNOWN: THINGS I WISH I'D UNDERSTOOD BEFORE I HIT THIRTY: COMPILED FROM ANSWERS TO A HIGHLY INFORMAL SURVEY ASKED OF PEOPLE OLDER AND POSSIBLY WISER THAN YOU

"Sunscreen and cocktails: one I should have used more, the other less."

"Get your mother's chicken soup recipe before it's too late."

"Exercise is a lovely habit, that started early, will last throughout your lifetime."

"I wish I had known in my twenties how quickly they would go by. I thought they would last forever. I wish I had set more goals, because I was just sort of drifting through my twenties, and all of a sudden I found myself turning thirty and picking up speed."

"One thing I wish I had known: to keep my blasted bell-bottoms securely fastened, because boy-craziness is not just a harmless foible—it is as dangerous and potentially destructive as a fondness for crack. Also: start saving money when you are about two, and never stop saving it."

"Never pass up an imperfect opportunity."

"Realize you will be working for the next fifty years. Make it important and meaningful to yourself. If possible, do something

that makes you feel great, because you'll have to get up every one of those work days."

"Righty-tighty, Lefty-loosey." (Author's note: Okay, this is the trick to help you remember that when you screw something in, you go to the right, and when you unscrew it, you go to the left. Honestly, I never learned this until I was well past my twenties, but it really does come in handy.)

"Don't think that you are the only one who feels like a fake sometimes—everyone does."

"I think that I would have to say cherish and celebrate sex. Not necessarily have more partners, but maybe have more nookie. It seems like it is all over the place and always will be, and then one day that isn't true anymore."

"I wish I had realized how much having a parent with an alcohol problem—not just someone who likes a couple of glasses of wine or a couple of beers once in a while—but someone who uses alcohol as an emotional crutch—an alcoholic—would impact my life and my relationships. I've realized how my expectations in relationships were formed by having an alcoholic mother, and a father who enabled it by allowing it to go on: I grew up believing that people will do irrational things and I just had to accept that and work with it. So, for example, when my husband told me that his infatuations were like being hit with a truck and there was nothing he could do about it, I believed that I had no control over it; that changing my behavior would not affect our relationship or his attractions outside the marriage, because changing my

behavior did nothing to change my mother's drinking and ugly, embarrassing, often hurtful outbursts. Of course it wouldn't, my behavior had nothing to do with her drinking. Alcoholics' primary relationship is with alcohol, which is really hard for the person who loves the alcoholic to come to terms with."

"If I had known I was going to be so happy in my fifties, I wouldn't have spent my twenties being so depressed."

"Don't marry anyone who doesn't want to marry you."

"Check yourself before you walk out the door. Lean your back against a wall, stand up straight, and get out there. You will look thinner, your clothes will fit better, and you will look confident even if you're not."

"The older I get, the more I realize how little I know and how much I still need—and want—to learn."

"Make sure you want to be married more than you want to get married."

"I wish I could have accepted myself for who I was because I suffered, worrying about what people thought of me."

"I wish I knew more about sex, about becoming a woman and all that goes along with that. I learned about getting my period from a book that mom told my sister to give me to read. Then I fell off my bike onto the bar and started bleeding. Obviously I hadn't read the book. I thought I'd really injured myself and was really

*freaked out. Ends up I got my period. Who knew? Certainly not
me."*

*"I wish I had just relaxed more about everything and that I wasn't
so hard on myself."*

"I know now that I can always trust my intuition."

*"In my twenties I tried very hard to not be like my parents. I
thought I had a completely different set of values. What I did
not realize is that much of my outlook, attitude, and fears were
actually traits that my parents handed down to me, traits that had
been passed down to them by their parents. Once I understood
that, it was both easy and cleansing to forgive my parents for being who they were and for holding the values they held. A belief
system is a hard thing to wrap one's mind around because it is
comprised of hundreds of little beliefs (such as 'show business is
all luck,' 'only Nazis wear brown shirts,' 'happiness always comes
with a price'). In my late twenties I began to realize that I had
much more control over my outlook and moods than I had ever
thought possible, and I remember thinking I wish I had known
this when I was younger; I might have spared myself a great deal
of teenage and twentysomething angst. Beware of the things that
motivate you, they may come from childhood beliefs that are no
longer appropriate, necessary, or helpful to the modern-day version of yourself."*

*"I would solicit and encourage advice from my peers; I would
think big and sometimes pretend I already am what I want to be.*

And most important I would judge people by their actions and not by their words."

"I sure wish someone had told me that life is hard. I didn't know that hardships and difficulties are a part of life, though I certainly experienced them. I thought they reflected on me, they happened because I screwed up or was screwed up. Now I know that if things don't go perfectly well—well, that's just a part of life. Everyone experiences difficulties of many kinds, and we're all subject to failures and grief along with the good times. It's just life!"

"I would have liked to have known that I didn't really know anything."

"I wish I hadn't waited until I was forty-five to go into therapy."

"I wish I had known when I was in my twenties that a person actually has to do things to make things happen. I believed, without thinking too much about it, that good things would just happen to me. I believed that God, or my guardian angel, or maybe it was my fairy godmother, would look after me, find me a good job, a good husband, a good house, a good life, and I just had to wait around for that to take place. It wasn't till maybe my late twenties that I sort of figured out that I was supposed to take some steps to make these things happen."

"Try to think why you're keeping people in your life who make you feel bad. There are more fish in the sea, and you're probably a nice person, you deserve nice people in your life."

A RATHER RANDOM BUT EXCELLENT BOOK LIST FROM THE
LOVELY LADIES OF BOOK GROUP

Amis, Kingsley – *Lucky Jim*

Atkinson, Kate – *The Human Croquet*

Austen, Jane – *Persuasion, Sense and Sensibility, Pride and Prejudice*

Becker, Ernest – *Denial of Death, Escape from Evil*

Bulgakov, Mikhail – *The Master and Margarita*

Camus, Albert – *The Plague*

Cary, Joyce – *The Horse's Mouth*

Coetzee, J. M. – *Waiting for the Barbarians*

Dawkins, Richard – *The Selfish Gene*

DeWitt, Helen – *The Last Samurai*

Dostoevsky, Fyodor – *Crime and Punishment*

Eliot, George – *Middlemarch*

Fielding, Henry – *Tom Jones*

Fowler, Henry W. – *Modern English Usage, The King's English*

Greene, Graham – *Travels with My Aunt*

Gurganus, Allan – *The Oldest Living Confederate Widow Tells All*

Hardy, Thomas – *Tess of the d'Urbervilles, The Mayor of Casterbridge*

Hugo, Victor – *Les Misérables*

Ishiguro, Kazuo – *The Unconsoled, Remains of the Day*

Levi, Primo – *Survival in Auschwitz*

Malamud, Bernard – *The Fixer*

Mann, Thomas – *Doctor Faustus*

Mitford, Nancy – *The Pursuit of Love*

Nabokov, Vladimir – *Lolita, Pale Fire*

Percy, Walker –*The Last Gentleman*

Potok, Chaim – *The Chosen*

Roth, Philip – *Portnoy's Complaint*

Rushdie, Salman – *Midnight's Children*

Sebald, W. G. – *The Rings of Saturn*

Shaw, George Bernard – *The Quintessence of Ibsenism*

Sobel, Dava – *Longitude*

Tremain, Rose – *Music and Silence*

Wallace, David Foster – *Infinite Jest*

Wharton, Edith – *The Age of Innocence*

Wodehouse, P. G. – *Code of the Woosters*

In Conclusion

I just have a few more things to say and then I'll shut up, because honestly, we've all got things to do, don't we? Just know that you will not know everything there is to know before the age of twenty-five. Keep your mind open and in a perpetual spongelike state, and live a life, so that you will have stories to tell when you are too old to do much of anything else. Keeping your mind active is not just good advice for those in the over-sixty set. Why not start now? Learn some new stuff, and develop strong opinions. Be prepared to change them, but don't be namby-pamby. Stand for something, and stand up for what you believe.

Too many of us buy into preconceptions we developed about ourselves as children or teenagers. "I'm hopeless at math," or "I've never been very handy," or "I'm not very musical," can define us for the rest of our lives. But just because someone once told you that you were terrible at spelling, or cooking, or drawing, or writing, or singing, or science, doesn't mean that you have to believe it. You have the rest of your lives to prove old adages wrong.

Be a kind and thoughtful person. Don't forget to drink water and wear a hat in the sun, but don't always come inside when it's raining. Splash in a few puddles and enjoy the showers, so you'll appreciate the sunshine that much more.

Acknowledgments

I would like to gratefully acknowledge the following helpful people, who all contributed, in one way or another, to the completion of this book:

Thank you to Richard Goldman, for the usual comments and great title; to my enthusiastic and very smart editor Cassie Jones, who totally gets it; thanks also to Mary Ellen O'Neill, Sabrina Faludi, and Johnathan Wilber; to my passionate and always-supportive agent Leslie Daniels; to the ever-perfect Geri Knorr for her helpful hints; and to my favorite financial know-it-alls, Robert Doig and Gail Neuman; and to all those friends who gave me their two cents and inspiration: Henry Spurgeon, Michael Andreen, Wendy DeRaud, Jane Mellor, Toni DeVito, Janet Travers, Martha French, Deborah Holland, Susanna Thompson, Gail Simmons, Clara Rodriguez, Phil Noyes, Tara Donato, Laurel Ollstein, Alicia Brandt, Maria Bustillos, Frankie Blue, Erik Knorr, the charming ladies of Book Group, and please be kind if I neglected to mention you by name; and thanks especially to those of you who where raised by wolves, for your understanding, good humor, and for providing such unending inspiration.

About the Author

Christie Mellor, author of *The Three-Martini Playdate: A Practical Guide to Happy Parenting* and *The Three-Martini Family Vacation: A Field Guide to Intrepid Parenting,* has been quoted in the *New York Times, San Francisco Chronicle,* and *Atlantic Monthly,* among others, and has received enthusiastic reviews from dozens of publications, including *Newsweek, People, Us Magazine, Playboy, Chicago Sun-Times, The Times* (of London), *Publishers Weekly,* and *Conde Nast Traveler.* Christie pursues a happy life in Los Angeles with her songwriter/copywriter husband, two almost-always pleasant boys, and a couple of high-strung ducks. She occasionally works as an actress and voice-over artist, likes to draw, and enjoys her martinis extremely well-chilled. Visit her colorful Web site: www.christiemellor.com.